Winning your benefit appeal

What you need to know

Child Poverty Action Group

Published by Child Poverty Action Group
30 Micawber Street
London N1 7TB
Tel: 020 7837 7979
staff@cpag.org.uk
www.cpag.org.uk
© Child Poverty Action Group 2016

A CIP record for this book is available from the British Library.
ISBN: 978 1 910715 16 1

Child Poverty Action Group is a charity registered in England and Wales (registration
number 294841) and in Scotland (registration number SC039339), and is a company
limited by guarantee, registered in England (registration number 1993854). VAT number:
690 808117

Cover design by Colorido Studios
Typeset by David Lewis XML Associates Ltd
Content management system by KonnectSoft
Printed and bound in the UK by CPI Group (UK) Ltd

Author
Simon Osborne is a welfare rights worker at CPAG.

Acknowledgements
Many thanks are due to Jon Shaw from CPAG in Scotland and Judge Edward Jacobs for their contributions to the first edition of this book. Thanks also to Judith Paterson for her comments, Alison Key for her thorough editing and for managing the book's production, Anne Ketley for updating the index and Kathleen Armstrong for proofreading the text.

About Child Poverty Action Group

Child Poverty Action Group is a national charity that works on behalf of the one in four children in the UK growing up in poverty. We use our understanding of what causes poverty and the impact it has on children's lives to campaign for policies that will prevent and solve poverty – for good.

We provide trusted and expert information and advice for the welfare rights and advice community – online, and through our books, training and advice services. Our advice lines support thousands of advisers a year, helping them to give families the best information and advice. Our *Welfare Benefits and Tax Credits Handbook*, described as the 'adviser's bible', is used by Citizens Advice Bureaux, local authorities and law centres throughout the UK. We also keep advisers up to date with trends and changes in the social security system through bulletins and our highly regarded training courses and seminars.

Poverty affects one in four children in the UK today. When children grow up poor they miss out – and so do the rest of us. They miss out on the things most children take for granted: warm clothes, school trips, having friends over for tea. They do less well at school and earn less as adults. Any family can fall on hard times and find it difficult to make ends meet. But poverty is not inevitable. With the right policies every child can have the opportunity to do well in life, and we all share the rewards of having a stronger economy and a healthier, fairer society.

If you would like to join us to help end child poverty, please visit www.cpag.org.uk, or follow us on Facebook (www.facebook.com/cpaguk) and Twitter (@cpaguk).

Keeping up to date

Advisers can get the latest information on appeals procedure and caselaw by booking on a CPAG training course. We can also provide your workplace with in-house training. See www.cpag.org.uk/training for more information.

Our *Welfare Benefits and Tax Credits Handbook 2016/17*, published in April 2016, tells you all you need to know about entitlement to benefits and tax credits, and contains the latest information on appeals.

Getting advice

Your local Citizens Advice Bureau or other advice centre can give you advice and support on benefits. See www.citizensadvice.org.uk if you live in England or Wales, or www.cas.org.uk if you live in Scotland.

CPAG has an advice line for advisers.

For advisers in the UK:
Telephone: 020 7812 5231, Monday to Friday 10am to 12pm and 2pm to 4pm

For advisers in Scotland:
Telephone: 0141 552 0552, Monday to Thursday 10am to 4pm and Friday 10am to 12pm
Email: advice@cpagscotland.org.uk

Contents

Chapter 1
Introduction

This chapter covers:

1. What is an appeal?

2. Who is this guide for?

3. Which decisions can you appeal?

4. Representatives

5. How do you win your appeal?

What you need to know

- If you disagree with a decision about your benefit or tax credit, you may be able to appeal against it.

- Appeals against benefit and tax credit decisions are made to an appeal tribunal called the 'First-tier Tribunal'.

- Appeal tribunals are courts of law and must apply the law. However, they are not as formal as many courts and are not supposed to be intimidating. They are usually more concerned with establishing facts and considering evidence than with detailed disputes about the law.

- If you want to appeal, it is best to have a 'representative' if you can. You do not need to be legally qualified or a legal expert to represent yourself or someone else in an appeal.

- It is often worth appealing, as there is a good success rate. However, you may be able to avoid an appeal by providing further information or evidence.

1. What is an appeal?

If you disagree with a decision about your benefit or tax credit claim, you can ask the 'decision maker' to look at it again. The decision maker is an officer in the Department for Work and Pensions, HM Revenue and Customs or local authority.

If the decision maker looks at the decision again and you are still unhappy, you can ask an independent tribunal to reconsider the decision. This is an appeal. Usually, you must ask for a decision to be looked at again before you can appeal.

The tribunal that deals with benefit and tax credits appeals is called the 'First-tier Tribunal'. It can make any decision that the decision maker could have made. This means it can 'uphold' the original decision, confirming that it is correct, or it can 'allow' the appeal and make a different decision. In some cases, the tribunal's decision may be less favourable to you than the decision maker's.

The tribunal must apply the law: it cannot make exceptions that the law does not allow. Winning your appeal means showing the tribunal how the facts and evidence in your case mean that the relevant law, when properly applied, means that you are entitled to benefit.

2. Who is this guide for?

This guide is for anyone who wants to appeal to the 'First-tier Tribunal'. It is particularly for people with little, or no, experience. However, if you have some experience, you might also find it useful.

The information and advice in this guide is addressed to 'you' as the claimant. However, you can have a 'representative' to assist you with your appeal and to represent you at the tribunal, and this guide can also be used by her/him to help her/him work on your appeal.

What does this guide cover?

This guide covers what you need to know in order to take an appeal to the 'First-tier Tribunal'. It explains:

- what you should do to help you win your appeal
- the appeal process
- how to prepare for the appeal
- how to gather evidence and construct your arguments
- how to write a 'submission'
- what happens at the appeal hearing

It is also possible to appeal against the First-tier Tribunal's decision. This appeal is made to a different tribunal, called the 'Upper Tribunal'. Appeals to the Upper Tribunal are more concerned with the interpretation of the law. This guide does not cover appeals to the Upper Tribunal, although there is some basic information about them in Chapter 7.

3. Which decisions can you appeal?

You can appeal about most decisions on your entitlement to social security benefits and tax credits, including:

- employment and support allowance, including whether or not you are fit for work
- jobseeker's allowance, including having your benefit 'sanctioned' for not taking part in an interview or not seeking work
- personal independence payment and disability living allowance
- universal credit
- housing benefit
- child tax credit and working tax credit
- the residence tests that apply to most benefits and tax credits

There are a few decisions that you cannot appeal against – eg, decisions about how and when a benefit or tax credit is paid and, if you have been overpaid tax credits or universal credit, whether the overpayment can be recovered from you.

Before you can appeal, you must usually have asked the 'decision maker' to look at the decision again. This is called a 'mandatory reconsideration'. There is information about this in Chapter 3.

What are most appeals about?

Currently, over three-quarters of benefit appeals are about illness or disability, and concern entitlement to personal independence payment or employment and support allowance. Most of the examples in this guide are therefore about these two benefits. Although appeals about personal independence allowance and employment and support allowance are essentially the same as appeals about other benefits, they involve particular issues about medical evidence and the tests that decide whether or not you qualify, including whether you are fit for work. Chapter 5 covers some of the issues that arise in these appeals.

4. Representatives

You can have a 'representative' to assist you with your appeal and help you put your case to the tribunal.

A representative does not need to be a lawyer or have a legal, or any other, qualification. However, the tribunal expects her/him to:

- know your case and the points s/he wishes to make
- help establish the facts
- have a basic knowledge of the relevant law

What CPAG says

Having a representative

It is always better to have a representative, if you can. S/he can provide a lot of help with preparing your appeal and increase the chances of your winning it.

A good representative is likely to have access to information and resources to help with the appeal, and may have some useful experience in representing other people. S/he can liaise on your behalf with the various official bodies involved in your appeal, and may be able to get evidence for you and write a 'submission' to send to the tribunal.

You do not have to have a representative and you can represent yourself in your appeal if you wish, or you can get help from a friend or relative. However, having a representative involves more than just having someone with you for reassurance or emotional support (valuable though these things are). A representative must present your case to the tribunal in the most effective way. So a good representative will help prepare your appeal by gathering relevant facts and evidence, checking the law and helping you get ready for the hearing.

If you do not have a representative, the tribunal does not expect you to do her/his job. Instead, it asks you about the basic facts in your case, such as your medical condition and what happened at your medical assessment.

Box A

Finding a representative

Most representatives are not lawyers or legally qualified. They are often people working for an advice centre, local authority, support group or charity, either as a paid worker or volunteer.

Representatives often work in:

- Citizens Advice Bureaux
- law centres
- firms of solicitors doing social security work
- local authority welfare rights units
- local disability charities or support groups
- unemployed workers' centres or trade unions
- hospitals and social services departments

More information about the role of representatives is in Chapter 4.

5. How do you win your appeal?

Is it worth appealing?

It is often worth appealing. Success rates are good, although they vary depending on the benefit concerned, whether there is an 'oral hearing' of the appeal and whether you are represented. Many decisions are matters of judgement or opinion, and another view of the same facts and evidence could be made. Sometimes, things simply go wrong.

Box B

Decisions worth appealing: examples

- A decision about the 'work capability assessment' that determines whether you are fit for work for employment and support allowance and universal credit. The official medical report may be inaccurate, or the 'decision maker' may have ignored evidence or not obtained evidence from someone who knows you.

- A decision about the disability tests for personal independence payment, disability living allowance and attendance allowance. The official medical report may be inaccurate, or the decision maker may have ignored evidence or not obtained evidence from someone who knows you.

- A decision involving the decision maker's judgement, such as whether you are living with another person as a couple, whether you deliberately got rid of money in order to get benefit, or whether you have a 'right to reside' in the UK.

- A decision involving a complex legal issue, which the decision maker may have misunderstood or wrongly applied.

However, there is no point appealing against a decision that is clearly legally correct, as this cannot be changed by the tribunal. For example, you may be disappointed by the amount of benefit you are paid, but if your award has been calculated correctly, the tribunal is bound by the law that sets the benefit rates and cannot change the decision.

Successful appeals

The overall success rate for all benefit and tax credit appeals is currently 56 per cent. This varies according to the benefit involved. The success rate is 61 per cent for personal independence payment appeals and 58 per cent for employment and support allowance appeals. Success rates are generally higher for claimants who attend their appeal hearing (an 'oral hearing'), and lowest if the appeal is decided just on the basis of the appeal papers (a 'paper hearing').

Success rates tend to be higher still if a 'representative' has helped with the appeal. Many representatives report success rates at oral hearings of 70 per cent or more.

To increase your chance of success, do the following.

- Ask for an oral hearing of your appeal, which you attend so that the tribunal can ask you questions, clarify facts and discuss the evidence.

- Have a representative, if possible. S/he can help check the law, gather evidence, write a 'submission', and assist you and the tribunal at the hearing.

- Be well prepared. Understand what the tribunal is like and what it can do. Be ready to answer any questions it may have.

Can an appeal be avoided?

An appeal is often necessary to correct an inaccurate or poor decision. However, as appeals are time consuming for everyone involved and can be stressful, you should consider whether an appeal can be avoided. The most effective way of avoiding an appeal is to make the 'decision maker' aware of information or evidence that s/he did not use when s/he made her/his original decision. For example, you could correct something that was misunderstood in a medical examination, provide supportive medical evidence from your

GP or provide evidence that your income is different from that used by the decision maker. Decision makers are trained to be prepared to consider such information or evidence, even after they have made their decision, and to change their initial decision if appropriate.

> Box C
> **Avoiding an appeal**
>
> • Is the decision wrong, or can you at least argue that it is wrong? For example, is it based on a judgement that could be challenged? Is it based on facts that have been misunderstood? If the decision is clearly correct, the tribunal cannot change it.
>
> • Is there an obvious simple mistake in the decision that can be pointed out to the decision maker, which clearly means the decision should be changed without the need for an appeal?
>
> • Is there any further information or evidence that might persuade the decision maker to change her/his decision without the need for an appeal?
>
> • If you must ask for the decision to be looked at again before you can appeal, is there further information or evidence that you could send with this request, so that the decision is changed without the need for an appeal?

If you must ask for the decision to be looked at again before you can appeal (a 'mandatory reconsideration'), this provides an opportunity to send further information or evidence.

Note: you can still provide further information or evidence after the appeal has been made.

Chapter 2
The appeals system

This chapter covers:

1. Who deals with your appeal?

2. Who is on the tribunal?

3. Where does the appeal take place?

4. What decisions can the tribunal make?

5. How long does the appeal process take?

What you need to know

- Tribunals are independent courts of law, but are not as formal as many courts.

- There is always a legally qualified judge on the tribunal and up to two other members. A tribunal clerk administers the appeal.

- The tribunal hearing is usually held in a venue in a nearby town or city.

- The tribunal reconsiders the decision being appealed. It can confirm or change it, and can even make a less favourable decision.

- Tribunals cannot award costs or compensation.

- Large numbers of appeals are received and dealt with every year, and the process is likely to take several months.

1. Who deals with your appeal?

Appeals are administered by HM Courts and Tribunals Service. The tribunal itself is called the 'First-tier Tribunal'. It is independent and has between one and three members. A clerk assists with the administration.

HM Courts and Tribunals Service

The appeals system overall is administered by HM Courts and Tribunals Service. This is an agency of the Ministry of Justice. Although it is a government body, it is independent of the organisations that make the initial decisions on your benefits and tax credits, such as the Department for Work and Pensions and HM Revenue and Customs. The people who sit on the tribunals are completely independent of all government departments.

The First-tier Tribunal

The 'First-tier Tribunal' considers appeals against decisions by:

- the Department for Work and Pensions about benefits such as employment and support allowance, personal independence payment, disability living allowance, jobseeker's allowance and universal credit
- HM Revenue and Customs about child benefit, guardian's allowance and tax credits
- local authorities about housing benefit

For administrative purposes, the First-tier Tribunal is organised into a number of different 'chambers' to hear different sorts of appeals. The chambers have different membership and sometimes slightly different rules. Social security and tax credit appeals are always included in the 'Social Entitlement Chamber' of the First-tier Tribunal. So if you come across a reference to the Social Entitlement Chamber, this refers to the type of tribunal that considers social security and tax credit appeals.

What does the tribunal clerk do?

The tribunal clerk deals with the administration of your appeal. S/he sends out the papers relating to the appeal, sets the date for the hearing and assists the tribunal with the administration on the day of the hearing. Clerks can also make some decisons in the run-up to the hearing – eg, about whether your appeal has been properly made. In practice, you deal with the clerk quite a lot before the hearing, so it is important to have a good working relationship with her/him.

2. Who is on the tribunal?

Members of the tribunal

The tribunal is made up of one, two or three members, depending on the type of appeal. There is always at least a legally qualified member, called the 'judge'.

Depending on the type of appeal, there may also be a medically qualified member and a disability qualified member.

Practice Statement of the Senior President of Tribunals, 'Composition of Tribunals in Social Security and Child Support Cases in the Social Entitlement Chamber on or after 1 August 2013'

The judge

The judge of the tribunal must be legally qualified. Usually this means that s/he is a solicitor or barrister with at least five years' experience. S/he knows about the law relevant to your appeal, but is not required to have worked in social security – eg, s/he may have worked as a solicitor in family or criminal law.

The judge chairs the hearing and provides the legal expertise for the tribunal.

The medically qualified member

This medically qualified member provides the medical expertise for the tribunal. S/he must be a registered medical practitioner. Usually s/he is a doctor, such as a GP, but need not have specialist knowledge in the area relevant to your appeal. S/he is not required to have a legal qualification. S/he may also carry out medical examinations for the Department for Work and Pensions medical service (currently contracted out to three companies: Maximus, Capita and Atos), but will not have previously been involved in the decision you are appealing.

The disability qualified member

The disability qualified member provides expertise about the effects of disability. S/he must be experienced in dealing with disability, either through having a disability her/himself, being a carer or working with people with disabilities – eg, as a physiotherapist, occupational therapist or social worker. S/he cannot be a doctor. Disability qualified members are not required to have a legal qualification.

The composition of the tribunal

What the law says

Tribunal composition

- **A three-person tribunal**, comprising a judge, a medically qualified member and a disability qualified member, hears appeals about disability living allowance, personal independence payment and attendance allowance.

- **A two-person tribunal**, comprising a judge and a medically qualified member, hears appeals about the 'work capability assessment' for employment and support allowance and universal credit, and about industrial injuries disablement benefit (unless it is about a declaration of an industrial accident).

- **A judge sitting alone** hears all other appeals.

Practice Statement of the Senior President of Tribunals, 'Composition of Tribunals in Social Security and Child Support Cases in the Social Entitlement Chamber on or after 1 August 2013'

The rules on the composition of the tribunal are fixed in law, and you cannot ask for a differently comprised tribunal. There are some exceptions.

- If your case is about a legal question and the medical and disability members are not necessary, a judge may hear the appeal alone.

- There can be a second doctor if your appeal involves complex medical issues, particularly in an industrial injuries disablement benefit case.

- If your case involves examining financial accounts, an accountant may sit with the judge to hear the appeal.

- If your appeal involves complex medical issues, but is not about a benefit that requires a two- or three-person panel, the tribunal could also include a doctor.

- A hearing can go ahead without one or more of the members usually required, but there must always be a judge present.

Have you got more than one appeal?

What the law says

Appeals about more than one benefit

Limited capability for work and personal independence payment/ disability living allowance appeals should be heard in 'completely separate sessions by completely differently composed tribunals'.

Upper Tribunal decision MB and Others v Secretary of State for Work and Pensions (ESA and DLA) [2013] UKUT 111 (AAC)

You may have appealed against decisions about different benefits, and so may have more than one appeal underway at the same time.

In general, your appeals are considered separately, but they can be considered during the same tribunal session – ie, on the same day. However, if your appeals are about personal independence payment and employment and support allowance, they must be heard by completely different tribunals in different sessions.

> **EXAMPLES**
>
> ### Tribunals hearing more than one appeal
>
> Ron has appealed against a decision refusing him personal independence payment. He has also appealed against a decision refusing him employment and support allowance because he fails the 'work capability assessment'.
>
> Ron's two appeals are heard by the 'First-tier Tribunal'. Even though the issues in them overlap because they both concern how Ron's illness affects him, the tribunals that consider them must be different: a three-person tribunal for the personal independence payment appeal and a two-person tribunal for the employment and support allowance appeal. The appeals must be completely separate – they must be considered in different sessions and by tribunals comprising different people.
>
> Joan has appealed against a decision refusing her personal independence payment. She has also appealed against a decision disqualifying her from contribution-based jobseeker's allowance for a period for leaving her job without 'just cause'.
>
> Joan's two appeals are heard by the First-tier Tribunal. The tribunals that consider them must be different: a three-person tribunal for the personal independence payment appeal and a judge sitting alone for her jobseeker's allowance appeal. In practice, both appeals could be considered during the same tribunal session, but they are heard separately.

3. Where does the appeal take place?

There is no specific rule about where an appeal must be held. There are tribunal venues in many towns and cities. Some are purpose built, but many are in places like civic centres. The venue should be accessible for people with disabilities. When you are notified of the date of your appeal hearing, the letter includes details of the venue location and how to get there.

At the tribunal venue, there is usually a waiting room and a separate room in which the appeal hearing takes place. If you are anxious in the waiting room, you can ask whether there is a private room available, although these are not available at all venues.

If you have any particular needs at the venue (eg, for a hearing loop or because of mobility problems), tell the clerk. S/he will make sure that you can access and use the venue.

Chapter 6 has more information about the appeal hearing.

Are you unable to attend the venue?

In exceptional cases, if you are unable to attend the tribunal venue at any time, the hearing can take place somewhere else, such as in your home. This type of hearing is called a 'domiciliary hearing'. You can request a domiciliary hearing and your request must be properly considered.

What the law says

Domiciliary hearings

A request for a domiciliary hearing must be properly considered, and the decision explained, in order to comply with the right to a fair trial under Article 6 of the European Convention on Human Rights, or to show that the tribunal has acted fairly and justly.

Commissioner's decision CSIB/2751/2002; Upper Tribunal decision PM v Secretary of State for Work and Pensions (IB) [2013] UKUT 301 (AAC)

However, you do not have an automatic right to a domiciliary hearing and, in practice, HM Courts and Tribunals Service almost always wants the hearing to take place at a tribunal venue. If you want a domiciliary hearing, you (or someone authorised to act for you) should write to the tribunal clerk and include medical evidence, such as a letter from a doctor, showing why one is necessary.

It is also possible for a hearing to be conducted over the telephone or via a video link. This may be considered, for instance, if you want to take part in the hearing but cannot attend in person, or if you live in a remote area and would have to wait a long time for a venue to be arranged. However, you do not have an automatic right to this and, in practice, these arrangments are rarely used.

What CPAG says

Attending the hearing

In most cases, it is always better to attend a hearing of your appeal in person, if you can. This usually provides the best opportunity for you to communicate your case effectively. If you have a 'representative' who can attend the hearing with you, s/he can help you.

4. What decisions can the tribunal make?

The tribunal can either confirm or change the decision being appealed.

If the tribunal confirms the decision, it is not changed. This is called 'upholding' the decision.

If the tribunal changes the decision to give you what you have asked for, this is sometimes called 'allowing' your appeal.

EXAMPLE

Allowing an appeal

Seren appeals against the decision that she has failed the 'work capability assessment'. The tribunal considers that she has scored sufficient points to pass the assessment and so changes the decision. It allows her appeal.

Changing the decision means that the tribunal substitutes the decision being appealed with one it considers to be correct. However, it does not have to make exactly the decision you have asked for.

For example, it may change the decision about your entitlement to personal independence payment to give you the 'daily living component' at the rate you asked for, but not award you the 'mobility component'. This is sometimes called allowing your appeal 'in part'.

EXAMPLES

Allowing an appeal in part

Heidi appeals against the decision not to award her personal independence payment. The tribunal decides to change the decision being appealed to make an award of personal independence payment. However, the tribunal makes the award at a lower rate than Heidi asked for. It allows her appeal in part.

Ian appeals against the decision that he failed the work capability assessment and so is not entitled to employment and support allowance. He argues firstly, that he passes the work capability assessment and so is entitled to employment and support allowance and, secondly, that he should be awarded the 'support component'.

The tribunal allows Ian's appeal in part. It decides that he satisfies the work capability assessment (and so is entitled to employment and support allowance), but it does not agree that he meets the conditions for the support component, but should receive the 'work-related activity component' instead.

The tribunal can make or remake whatever decision could have been made by the 'decision maker'. Sometimes, this is described as 'standing in the decision maker's shoes': the tribunal is reconsidering the decision that is being appealed – nothing more and nothing less.

Can the tribunal make a less favourable decision?

Because it can make whatever decision could have been made by the 'decision maker', occasionally a tribunal may change a decision but make another that is less favourable to you than the one you appealed against.

For example, you may have appealed against being refused the 'daily living component' of personal independence payment, but you do not want the tribunal to change your award of the 'mobility component', because you are happy with this. However, because you are appealing against the decision about your overall entitlement to personal independence payment, and the decision maker could allow or refuse either or both components, the tribunal could 'uphold' the part of the decision about the care component and also remove the award of the mobility component.

This situation is uncommon, but can happen, particularly in appeals about illness and disability issues. Chapter 5 has more information on these.

Can the tribunal award compensation or costs?

The tribunal cannot change the law: it must apply the law as it stands. Because it is applying the social security or tax credit law, it has no power to look at complaints about administration.

The tribunal cannot award costs or damages to anyone involved in the appeal. So, for example, it cannot order that you be paid compensation, or that your and your 'representative's' costs be paid, or that you must pay someone else's costs.

> **EXAMPLE**
>
> ### What the tribunal can and cannot do
>
> Danny was refused the 'limited capability for work element' in his universal credit because he failed the 'work capability assessment'. He considered that his mobility problems meant that he should have passed this and so appealed against this decision. At the hearing, Danny tells the tribunal that he is unhappy about the medical examination he attended and felt the doctor asked him rude and unhelpful questions. He asks that he be paid compensation for his upset and inconvenience.
>
> The tribunal 'allows' Danny's appeal, because it considers that he scores sufficient points to satisfy the work capability assessment. So he is entitled to the limited capability for work element. However, the tribunal cannot award him any compensation for his bad experience at the medical examination – this was not part of the decision being appealed.

5. How long does the appeal process take?

HM Courts and Tribunals Service deals with a large number of appeals every year. Following a dramatic fall in the number of appeals after the introduction of 'mandatory reconsiderations' in 2013, the number is increasing again: 157,180 appeals were received in 2015/16.

The amount of time it takes from receiving an appeal at HM Courts and Tribunals Service to notifying you of the outcome is known as the 'clearance time'.

In 2015/16, the average clearance time for a social security appeal was 18 weeks. However, the time varies between different benefits: tribunals comprising a judge sitting alone (eg, a jobseeker's allowance appeal) can take less time to clear than average; tribunals with other members (eg, an employment and support allowance appeal) can take more time to clear than average.

Clearance times also vary between different parts of the country. If you have a 'representative', s/he may know how long the appeal process takes in your area and be able to advise you how long you are likely to have to wait.

What CPAG says

Waiting for your appeal

You can expect to wait at least several weeks, possibly several months, for your appeal to be decided.

This waiting time can be very difficult, as you are likely to be in financial need, and your circumstances may change while you are waiting for your appeal – eg, your health may worsen or improve. Get advice about which benefits you might be able to get while you are waiting for your appeal to be dealt with.

You can ask the tribunal clerk to try to ensure that your appeal is heard as early as possible – sometimes this is called 'expediting' your appeal. Try to provide particular reasons why your appeal needs to be heard quickly – eg, if your health is at risk or if you may be evicted from your home.

Further information

There is a tribunal 'venue finder' at www.justice.gov.uk/tribunals/sscs/venues.

Chapter 3
Making an appeal

This chapter covers:

1. Can you appeal?

2. Which decisions can be appealed?

3. What is a mandatory reconsideration?

4. Is there a time limit for appealing?

5. How do you make a valid appeal?

What you need to know

- You can appeal against most benefit and tax credit decisions.

- Except for housing benefit, before you can appeal you must ask for the decision to be looked at again and have your request considered. This is called a 'mandatory reconsideration'.

- You must appeal within one month of the date of the decision, although in some circumstances this can be extended.

- Your appeal must be made in writing and contain certain information, including your reasons ('grounds') for the appeal.

- Appeals following a mandatory reconsideration are made directly to HM Courts and Tribunals Service. Housing benefit appeals are made to the local authority that made the decision.

1. Can you appeal?

Before you can appeal against a benefit or tax credit decision, the following must apply.

- You must have been sent a 'decision notice'.

- The decision must have the 'right of appeal' – ie, it must be one that you can appeal.

- Unless it is a housing benefit decision, the 'decision maker' must have looked at the decision again. This is called a 'mandatory reconsideration'. S/he must have made a decision about this and sent it to you in a 'mandatory reconsideration notice'.

Have you been sent a decision notice?

Once you have made a valid claim for a benefit or tax credit, your claim is referred to a 'decision maker'. The decision maker decides whether or not you are entitled.

If the decision is one you can appeal, you must be sent a written notice informing you of the decision and of your right to appeal. You can appeal against most decisions.

Unless it is a housing benefit decision, this 'decision notice' also tells you that you must ask for the decision to be looked at again before you can appeal.

Decision notices about universal credit may be sent to your online account, rather than through the post.

Decisions about employment and support allowance or personal independence payment usually include details of the number of points you have been awarded in your medical assessment. Decisions about 'means-tested benefits' (eg, universal credit) and tax credits usually contain details of how your entitlement has been calculated, including what income or capital has been taken into account.

If you are already getting a benefit or tax credit and your circumstances change (eg, your income increases or decreases, or your health improves or deteriorates), this can mean a new decision on your entitlement is made. You are sent a decision notice telling you about the change in your entitlement and informing you of your right to appeal and (except for housing benefit) that you must ask for the decision to be looked at again before you can appeal.

Decision notices can vary, but they are always:

- in writing
- from a decision maker
- about your entitlement to benefit or tax credits

You can appeal against any part of a decision notice about your entitlement.

Who else can appeal?

Benefit or tax credit claimants can appeal. In addition, the following people can appeal against a decision about all benefits and tax credits, except housing benefit:

- someone authorised to act on your behalf (known as an 'appointee')
- someone claiming personal independence payment, disability living allowance or attendance allowance on your behalf if you are terminally ill (even if this is without your knowledge)
- someone from whom an 'overpayment' of benefit, a 'short-term advance' of benefit, a 'budgeting advance' of universal credit or 'hardship payments' can be recovered – eg, if the overpayment was caused by her/him
- your partner, if the decision concerns whether s/he failed to take part in a 'work-focused interview' without having a good cause
- someone appointed by the Department for Work and Pensions or HM Revenue and Customs to proceed with a claim for benefit for someone who has died

The following people can appeal against a decision about housing benefit:

- someone acting for you because you cannot act yourself – eg, an appointee
- someone from whom an overpayment can be recovered – eg, your landlord
- a landlord or agent if it has been decided to make (or not to make) payments of housing benefit directly to you

2. **Which decisions can be appealed?**

Most decisions about benefits and tax credits, including all decisions about your entitlement, can be appealed. This is sometimes called 'carrying the right of appeal'.

Appeal rights	
Decision	Can you appeal?
Your employment and support allowance is stopped because you failed the 'work capability assessment'	Yes
You are not awarded the 'support component' in your employment and support allowance or the 'limited capability for work-related activity element' in your universal credit	Yes
Your care and mobility needs are regarded as not sufficient to get personal independence payment	Yes
You cannot be paid by cheque	No
You cannot be paid a 'budgeting advance'	No
You do not satisfy the 'right to reside' test	Yes
The amount of your housing benefit is reduced because of the number of bedrooms you have	Yes
The amount of your benefit is reduced because you did not take part in a 'work-focused interview'	Yes
Your income is too high for universal credit	Yes
You have been overpaid benefit or tax credits	Yes
An 'overpayment' of universal credit or tax credits will be recovered from you	No

Some decisions cannot be appealed. These are usually about the way your benefit or tax credit is paid, such as when or how payments are made. A few specific decisions, such as about entitlement to a 'short-term advance' of benefit or a budgeting advance of universal credit, cannot be appealed.

The 'decision notice' informing you of your entitlement states whether you have a right to appeal. If you think that you can appeal, but the 'decision maker' does not, ask for your appeal to be forwarded to HM Courts and Tribunals Service. You should state clearly why you believe you have a right to appeal against the decision in question.

Can decisions about overpayments be appealed?

What the law says

Appeals about overpayments

A decision that you have been overpaid can be appealed, because it is a decision about your entitlement.

In most cases, a decision about whether an overpayment of benefit can be recovered from you can also be appealed. However, a decision about recovering overpayments of universal credit and contributory employment and support allowance and contribution-based jobseeker's allowance paid under the universal credit system cannot be appealed. Instead, you must dispute this with the decision maker at the Department for Work and Pensions.

A decision about whether an overpayment of tax credits can be recovered from you cannot be appealed. Instead, you must dispute this with the decision maker at HM Revenue and Customs.

Section 71ZB Social Security Administration Act 1992; section 38 Tax Credits Act 2002

If you have been paid more benefit or tax credits than you are entitled to, this is called an 'overpayment'. You should be sent a decision changing your entitlement to the correct amount, telling you about the overpayment and saying whether or not you must pay it back – ie, whether it is 'recoverable' from you.

You can appeal about whether or not you have been overpaid. However, you do not always have the right to appeal about whether the overpayment can be recovered from you.

EXAMPLE

Appealing against an overpayment decision

Rashid has received a decision saying that he was not entitled to the universal credit he was paid during July and August, he has therefore been overpaid and that he must repay the money.

Rashid can appeal against the decision that he was not entitled to universal credit during July and August. He must ask for the decision to be looked at again (a 'mandatory reconsideration') first. However, he cannot appeal against the decision that he must repay the money he was paid during this time.

If Rashid accepts that he was not entitled to universal credit, although he cannot appeal about the recovery of the overpayment, he can dispute it with the Department for Work and Pensions. For example, he could argue that recovering the overpayment from him will cause him extreme hardship.

3. What is a mandatory reconsideration?

What the law says

Mandatory reconsideration

If a written benefits decision includes a statement that someone only has the right of appeal if the decision maker has considered an application to revise the decision, that person only has the right of appeal if the decision maker has 'considered, on an application, whether to revise the decision'.

An appeal may not be made against a tax credits decision unless 'a review of the decision has been carried out... and notice of the conclusion of the review has been given...'.

Regulation 7 The Universal Credit, Personal Independence Payment, Jobseeker's Allowance and Employment and Support Allowance (Decisions and Appeals) Regulations 2013; regulation 3ZA The Social Security and Child Support (Decisions and Appeals) Regulations 1999; section 38(1A) Tax Credits Act 2002

For most benefits (except housing benefit) and for tax credits, before you can appeal you must ask for the decision you are unhappy with to be looked at again. You must do so within a certain period of time and your request must be considered by a 'decision maker'. This is known as a 'mandatory reconsideration'.

When the decision maker reconsiders a benefit decision in this way, s/he carries out a 'revision'. When s/he reconsiders a tax credits decision, s/he carries out a 'review'.

You are sent a decision about the outcome of the mandatory reconsideration in a letter, usually called a 'mandatory reconsideration notice'. This tells you whether the decision you are unhappy about has been changed, or not. It also tells you about your right to appeal. The letter may not always have the words 'mandatory reconsideration notice' at the top, but the phrase usually appears in it. At this point, if you are still unhappy, you can appeal.

What CPAG says

Mandatory reconsideration

The Department for Work and Pensions says that before you can appeal, the decision maker must have considered your application for a mandatory reconsideration, carried out a revision and issued a new decision in a mandatory reconsideration notice. However, the law for benefits only requires the decision maker to have 'considered' your application. There is therefore currently dispute about whether you can appeal if the decision maker does not accept your application (eg, perhaps because you applied too late) and so does not actually carry out a revision and issue a new decision in a mandatory reconsideration notice. This point may be clarified by a court decision in the future. If you think you might be affected, get advice.

The law for tax credits is very clear: before you can appeal, a review must have been carried out and notice of this sent to you.

Box A

The mandatory reconsideration process

Step one: receive a 'decision notice' from the decision maker.

Step two: apply to the decision maker for the decision to be reconsidered.

Step three: receive a mandatory reconsideration notice.

Step four: send your appeal to HM Courts and Tribunals Service.

The mandatory reconsideration process does not apply to housing benefit. You can ask for a decision on your housing benefit to be looked at again if you wish before you appeal, but you do not have to.

What CPAG says

Housing benefit decisions

Asking for a housing benefit decision to be looked at again is one way of avoiding an appeal. The way in which you do this is the same as the way in which you apply for a mandatory reconsideration of a benefit decision. However, unless the local authority has made a very simple and obvious mistake in its decision, it may be better to appeal straight away. If you appeal, the local authority should look at the decision again anyway. If the local authority does not change its decision, the appeal will need to continue if you still want to get the decision changed.

Note: if you are already getting benefit or tax credits and your circumstances change (eg, your income increases), the decision awarding you benefit or tax credits may be looked at again. This is called a 'supersession' if it is about a benefit or a 'revision' if it is about tax credits. It is not a mandatory reconsideration and the new decision you get does not give you the right to appeal. If you are unhappy with the new decision you get following a change in your circumstances, before you can appeal you must ask for this to be looked at again in a mandatory reconsideration.

How do you apply for a mandatory reconsideration of a benefit decision?

You can request a 'mandatory reconsideration' of a benefit decision verbally (eg, over the telephone) or in writing. It is better to request it in writing, as you can keep a copy in case there is a dispute about whether, or when, you made the request. You do not have to use the words 'mandatory reconsideration' or 'revision'. The key point is that you ask for the decision to be looked at again. However, in practice, it is clearer if you ask specifically for a mandatory reconsideration.

Your request must be received by the 'decision maker' within one month of the date the decision was sent to you. If your request is made within this time limit, a mandatory reconsideration must then be carried out.

What the law says

Month

A month is a calendar month. For example, one calendar month from 1 June is 1 July.

Schedule 1 Interpretation Act 1978; paragraph 03063 Department for Work and Pensions Decision Makers' Guide

This basic time limit can be extended by 14 days if the decision did not contain a written 'statement of reasons' and you request one within the month. In practice, however, this rarely happens as most decisions are regarded as already including such a statement.

If you request a mandatory reconsideration within the time limit, you do not need to give any reasons (or 'grounds') for why the decision should be changed. This is sometimes called an 'any grounds revision'.

Applying for a mandatory reconsideration

Javed has received a decision saying that he is not entitled to employment and support allowance because he does not satisfy the 'work capability assessment'. The 'decision notice' is dated 1 June 2016. It contains a statement of reasons for the decision, explaining why he is not entitled.

Javed thinks he should have scored suffcient points to have passed the work capability assessment. On 25 June 2016, he phones the Department for Work and Pensions on the number on the decision notice and requests that the decision be looked at again. As he is within the one-month time limit, he does not need to prove anything more for a mandatory reconsideration to take place.

A decision maker at the Department for Work and Pensions accepts Javed's request and carries out a revision, but concludes that the original decision is correct and should not be changed. This decision is notified in writing to Javed in a 'mandatory reconsideration notice'. Javed can now appeal against the decision to the 'First-tier Tribunal'.

Have you missed the time limit?

If you want the decision to be looked at again, but you have missed the one-month time limit, it may still be possible to apply for a mandatory reconsideration. Make it clear that you are making a late request for a mandatory reconsideration. The decision maker can carry out a revision of the decision for any reason (on any grounds) if you make your request ask within:

- 13 months of the date you were notified of the decision
- 13 months of the date the one-month time limit expired if the decision is about personal independence payment or universal credit

Make sure you enable the decision to be identified in your application and include a summary of the reasons why it is late.

For a revision to be carried out on any grounds, the decision maker must be satisfied that it is reasonable to do so and there are special circumstances why you did not apply in time. 'Special circumstances' are not defined.

EXAMPLE

Applying for a late mandatory reconsideration

On 5 March 2016, Marion was sent a decision about her personal independence payment. This told her that she was not entitled to the 'mobility component' as she could walk and did not need anyone with her when she was outdoors.

Marion experiences extreme anxiety and depression, and the decision came at a bad time for her. She was too unwell to do anything about it until 10 June 2016, when she went to her local advice centre for help.

The advice centre helped her to make a late request for a mandatory reconsideration, explaining that it was late because Marion had been in a period of particular bad health after receiving the decision and had not been able to deal with any correspondence. It enclosed a letter from her GP confirming this. The adviser also pointed out in the letter that Marion's health problems have always meant that she needs a companion when she goes out – something that has been accepted in the past, and her health has not got any better.

The decision maker at the Department for Work and Pensions accepts Marion's late request. However, the decision maker confirms the original decision and so Marion still does not get the mobility component. Because a revision has been carried out, Marion is sent the decision in a mandatory reconsideration notice. She can now appeal to the First-tier Tribunal.

If your application for a late mandatory reconsideration is refused, a revision is not carried out and a mandatory reconsideration notice is not issued. The Department for Work and Pensions says that you cannot appeal.

It may be possible to make a late request for a mandatory reconsideration, even after the 13-month time limit. This is because in some very limited circumstances a revision can be carried out 'at any time' – ie, there is no time limit. This is known as an 'any time revision'.

The main situation when you may be able to do this is when there has been an 'official error' – ie, if the decision contains a mistake made by the Department for Work and Pensions, HM Revenue and Customs or local authority. If this applies to you, make it clear that you are making a late request for a mandatory reconsideration and that you believe the decision you are unhappy about is wrong because of an official error, so a revision can be carried out at any time. However, in practice, the Department for Work and Pensions may be unwilling to accept your request.

Box B
What is an official error?

The Department for Work and Pensions, HM Revenue and Customs or local authority can make an official error. This can be:

- a mistake about the law (but not if this is only because it has been shown to be wrong by a later 'Upper Tribunal' or court decision)
- a failure to take specific, relevant evidence into account
- a failure to pass written evidence it has received to the decision maker
- a failure to ask about something that is relevant (but not if it is about not keeping your claim under constant review, or not raising things not raised by you)

Box C
Time limits: checklist

- If you think you may want to appeal, ask for your decision to be looked at again (say that you want a mandatory reconsideration) within the one-month time limit. You are then guaranteed to get a mandatory reconsideration notice and have the right to appeal. You do not have to give any reasons for your request. However, make a strong case for why the decision should be changed, as this may mean an appeal can be avoided.

- If you have missed the time limit, you can make a late request within the 13-month period. The decision maker may refuse your request. If this is the case, a revision is not carried out and you may not be able to appeal, so give as much information as you can for why you are late and send evidence to support this.

- If you are making a late request after the 13-month period, check whether it is possible to have a revision at any time. In practice, this may only be the case if there has been an official error. The decision maker may refuse your request. If this is the case, a revision is not carried out and you may not be able to appeal.

How do you apply for a mandatory reconsideration of a tax credits decision?

You must request a 'mandatory reconsideration' of a tax credits decision in writing. It is best to use the official HM Revenue and Customs form *What To Do If You Think Your Child Tax Credit or Working Tax Credit Is Wrong* (WTC/AP), available from www.gov.uk. Send your request to HM Revenue and Customs at the address given on the 'decision notice'.

If you do not use the official form, make sure you identify the decision you are unhappy about. Although it is not essential, it is best to make it clear that you are asking for a mandatory reconsideration of the decision.

Your request must be received by HM Revenue and Customs within 30 days of the date given on the decision letter. If this is the case, a 'review' must be carried out.

If your request is late, explain why. HM Revenue and Customs may accept a late request, provided you make this within 13 months of the original decision and it is satisfied that there were special circumstances that meant it was not practical for you to meet the 30-day time limit. It must also be reasonable for HM Revenue and Customs to accept your late request. The longer the delay, the more compelling your reasons must be. There is no definitive list of reasons that may be accepted, so explain anything that meant your request was late – eg, if you were ill or recently bereaved, or if you have had problems dealing with correspondence or a domestic emergency.

If your application for a late review is not accepted, a review is not carried out and, therefore, you do not have a right to appeal.

Do you have a mandatory reconsideration notice?

If you have received a 'mandatory reconsideration notice' and you remain unhappy with the decision, you can appeal.

A 'mandatory reconsideration notice' is the letter from the Department for Work and Pensions or HM Revenue and Customs informing you that a decision has been looked at again and the outcome.

The letter is sent to you by post, or it may be sent to your online account if it is about universal credit. Not all letters contain the words 'mandatory reconsideration notice'. However, if you have a received a letter from the Department for Work and Pensions or HM Revenue and Customs confirming that you have asked for the decision to be looked at again and it has reconsidered it, this counts as a mandatory reconsideration notice and you have the right to appeal.

If the decision can be appealed, the mandatory reconsideration notice should say so. If the decision does not have a right of appeal, but you think it should have, HM Courts and Tribunals Service decides.

4. Is there a time limit for appealing?

What the law says

Time limits

The basic time limit is one month.

One month = one calendar month.

The absolute time limit for a late appeal is 13 months.

Rules 22 and 23 The Tribunal Procedure (First-tier Tribunal) (Social Entitlement Chamber) Rules 2008; commissioner's decision R(IB) 4/02

Your appeal must be made within a set time limit. This is one calendar month. The time limit starts from the date the decision in the 'mandatory reconsideration notice' was sent to you. If you want to appeal a housing benefit decision, your appeal must be received within one month of the date the original decision was issued or, if you asked for a 'revision', within one month of date the revision decision was issued.

EXAMPLE

Time limits

A mandatory reconsideration notice is sent to Charlie on 4 November. The original decision is not changed by the 'decision maker'. Charlie wants to appeal.

The basic time limit for Charlie to make his appeal expires at the end of 4 December – one calendar month from the date of the decision in the mandatory reconsideration notice. His appeal must be received by HM Courts and Tribunals Service before then.

This basic time limit can be extended by 14 days if the decision did not contain a written 'statement of reasons' and you request one within the month. However, in practice, this rarely applies as most decisions are regarded as already including such a statement.

Note: the appeal must be *received* within the time limit – it is not enough for you to have sent it in time.

Have you missed the time limit?

What the law says

Late appeals

The First-tier Tribunal decides whether an appeal can go ahead. It is not restricted in what it can take into account when making its decision.

In exceptional cases, an appeal outside the absolute time limit may need to be accepted.

Rules 22(8) and 23(4) The Tribunal Procedure (First-tier Tribunal) (Social Entitlement Chamber) Rules 2008; Upper Tribunal decision KK v Sheffield City Council (CTB) [2015] UKUT 367 (AAC)

If you do not appeal within the time limit, you may be able to make a late appeal. There is an absolute time limit of 13 months in which to do this. This 13-month period runs from the date the 'mandatory reconsideration notice' was sent to you. For housing benefit, it runs from the date of the original decision, or from the date the 'revision' decision was sent to you, if a revision was carried out.

If you request a late appeal, state this clearly in your letter or on the appeal form. Include the reasons why your appeal is late. 'Reasons' are not defined in the rules, but could include things like illness, a lack of advice or language problems. Also include why it is important for the appeal to go ahead – eg, the strength of your case and the amount of money at stake.

EXAMPLE

Requesting a late appeal

Morag received a decision, dated 21 May, saying that she was not entitled to personal independence payment. She disagreed with the decision and asked for it to be looked at again. Morag's request was received on 15 June. A 'mandatory reconsideration' was carried out, but the decision was not changed. A mandatory reconsideration notice containing the decision was sent to Morag on 9 July.

After getting the mandatory reconsideration notice, Morag had an accident at home which resulted in her spending a short time in hospital. Because of this, she does not appeal until 2 September. This is outside the basic one-month time, starting on 9 July, but within the absolute 13-month period.

Morag states on her appeal form that she is appealing late because her accident and hospital stay made it difficult for her to appeal with one month. She also explains that her appeal has strong merits and that her GP can confirm that she needs a lot of help at home and did so even before her accident.

The 'decision maker' at the Department for Work and Pensions does not object to the appeal going ahead. The tribunal decides to accept a late appeal and to consider whether Morag qualifies for personal independence payment.

The tribunal decides whether or not to allow your appeal to go ahead, not the Department for Work and Pensions, HM Revenue and Customs or local authority. It is not bound by any special rules, but must ensure that your request is considered 'fairly and justly'.

If the decision maker does not object, your appeal is allowed to go ahead, unless the tribunal decides otherwise. It is unusual for the tribunal to do this. Even if the decision maker objects, the tribunal can still decide that your appeal should go ahead. The tribunal may write to you and give you a chance to comment, before making its decision.

In exceptional circumstances (eg, if you did not receive the decision that you wish to appeal against), it may be possible to argue that you should still be able to make a late appeal even after the 13-month time limit. However, you must show that you did everything you could to appeal in time.

If the tribunal refuses to accept your appeal, it cannot go ahead. You can appeal against the refusal to the 'Upper Tribunal'.

5. How do you make a valid appeal?

Your appeal must be valid. This means it must satisfy certain conditions. If your appeal is not valid, it will be cancelled and not allowed to go ahead. This is called being 'struck out'.

What the law says

Valid appeals

To be valid, your appeal must:
- be in writing (in English or in Welsh)
- signed by you
- include certain information

A solicitor can sign an appeal for a claimant. A representative who is not a solicitor can also sign an appeal for a claimant, provided s/he has written authorisation.

Rules 22 and 23 The Tribunal Procedure (First-tier Tribunal) (Social Entitlement Chamber) Rules 2008; regulation 20 The Housing Benefit and Council Tax Benefit (Decisions and Appeals) Regulations 2001; Upper Tribunal decision CO v LB Havering [2015] UKUT 28 (AAC)

Your 'representative' can sign the appeal for you if s/he has your written authority, but to avoid complications it is best for you sign the appeal if you can.

Do you have to use the official appeal form?

It is not essential to use an official appeal form to make your appeal. However, it is advisable to do so, as it is the best way of ensuring that all the relevant information is included. A local authority may insist that you use its official appeal form, although the decision on whether your appeal is valid is always made by the tribunal, not the local authority.

Some advice agencies keep copies of the form. If you have a 'representative', s/he may have one.

Appeal forms		
Type of decision	Form	Available from
Most benefits	SSCS1	www.gov.uk/social-security-child-support-tribunal/appeal-tribunal
Housing benefit	local authority's own appeal form	local authority
Child benefit and guardian's allowance decisions made by HM Revenue and Customs	SSCS5	www.gov.uk/social-security-child-support-tribunal/appeal-tribunal
Tax credits	SSCS5	www.gov.uk/social-security-child-support-tribunal/appeal-tribunal

What information must be included?

You must include the following details.

- Your details, and those of your 'representative', if you have one.

- The 'grounds' of the appeal. This is a summary of the reasons why you think the decision is wrong. The appeal form usually has a large box to use for these details.

- The address where the appeal documents should be sent. This can be your representative's address, but check with her/him about this.

- Except in housing benefit appeals, a copy of the decision you are appealing. This is usually the 'mandatory reconsideration notice'.

- Except in housing benefit appeals, any documents in support of the appeal which the 'decision maker' does not already have.

If your appeal is about housing benefit, although you do not need to provide a copy of the decision being appealed, you must still identify it – eg, by giving its date.

The official appeal form from HM Courts and Tribunals Service also asks for additional information, such as your national insurance number and whether you would like an 'oral hearing'. If you request an oral hearing, there are further questions about the arrangements – eg, the dates you are unavailable and if you have any particular requirements at the tribunal venue, such as a hearing loop or an interpreter. The official appeal form from the local authority in housing benefit cases may ask for similar additional information.

Further details can always be provided at a later date.

What should you do if you cannot include all the required information?

The tribunal clerk can ignore (or 'waive') things that are normally required if this would be 'fair or just'. So, for example, if you do not have a copy of your 'mandatory reconsideration notice', send your appeal anyway in order not to miss the time limit and provide as many other details as possible – eg, the date of the original decision, evidence that you requested a 'mandatory reconsideration' and evidence that this was carried out. Ask the Department for Work and Pensions or HM Revenue and Customs for a copy of the mandatory reconsideration notice, and send it once you get it. However, the clerk is less likely to ignore the fact that you have not included basic information, such relevant names and addresses.

What are the grounds for your appeal?

The 'grounds' for your appeal are the reasons why you disagree with the decision.

Your grounds do not need to refer to the details of the law, but they must state why you are appealing and show why you think the decision is wrong.

- Grounds do not need to be lengthy, but should be as clear as possible. Just indicating your disagreement is probably not enough.

- Try to identify the particular reasons why the decision is wrong.

- Send any evidence you have in support of the appeal that the 'decision maker' does not have. Send this as soon as it is available, and keep a copy and a record of posting. If there is something obviously wrong with the evidence used to make the decision, such as an inadequate medical examination, say so.

EXAMPLE

Grounds for the appeal

'I am appealing against this decision because I think I am too ill to work because of my walking problems and arthritis, and so should be entitled to employment and support allowance.

- I can't walk more than about 20 metres without having to stop because I am so out of breath, and after that I can only walk about the same again before having to stop altogether. I don't use a wheelchair as I have not been recommended one by my doctor.

- Because of my arthritis I can't stand or sit for long before having to move about.'

EXAMPLE

Grounds for the appeal

'I disagree with the decision that I am not entitled to personal independence payment. I think I am entitled to the daily living part because of the amount of help I need during the day.

I put on the form that I need a lot of help with things like washing and dressing, and with cooking and eating, and with dealing with bills and letters – several times a day. I need a lot of prompting and encouragement to do these things because of my depression and anxiety. But the nurse I saw at the medical did not ask me much about this, and the decision seems to have ignored what I said.'

Where should you send your appeal?

Send your housing benefit appeal to the local authority that made the decision.

Otherwise, send your appeal to HM Courts and Tribunals Service. This is sometimes called 'direct lodgement'.

In England and Wales: HMCTS SSCS Appeals Centre, PO Box 1203, Bradford BD1 9WP.

In Scotland: HMCTS SSCS Appeals Centre, PO Box 27080, Glasgow G2 9HQ.

Is your appeal invalid?

Only the tribunal can decide whether or not your appeal is valid. If the tribunal clerk thinks there is not enough information in your appeal to make it valid, s/he can ask you to provide more. If you used the official appeal form, it is returned to you for more information to be added. It is important to comply as far as possible with what the clerk asks for. Otherwise, s/he may decide that your appeal is not valid and may cancel ('strike out') it.

If an appeal is struck out, it does not go ahead. If your appeal is struck out, you can ask the tribunal to reconsider the clerk's decision. Apply in writing within 14 days of the date you were notified of your appeal being struck out.

In housing benefit appeals, the local authority 'decision maker' can return the appeal form for completion or request that further information be supplied. If it does this, the basic time limit for appealing is extended by at least 14 days. If you do not comply with the local authority's request, it must forward the matter to the tribunal – only the tribunal can make the decision on whether your appeal is valid.

Further information

For more details about getting benefit and tax credit decisions changed, see CPAG's *Welfare Benefits and Tax Credits Handbook*.

Chapter 4
Preparing your appeal

This chapter covers:

1. What are tribunals like?

2. Do you have a representative?

3. How do you prepare your appeal?

4. What is the point of the appeal?

5. How do you check the law?

6. How do you gather facts and evidence?

7. How do you write a submission?

What you need to know

- Tribunals are 'inquisitorial'. This means they are concerned with establishing facts and considering evidence in order to establish the truth.

- It is strongly advisable to have a 'representative' to help you with your appeal, if you can.

- Preparing for your appeal involves checking the law, gathering relevant facts and evidence, and writing a brief 'submission'.

- You do not have to submit further evidence or a written submission for your appeal, but doing so usually increases your chances of winning.

1. What are tribunals like?

What the law says

The nature of tribunals

The overriding objective of the tribunal rules is to ensure that cases are dealt with 'fairly and justly'. This includes 'avoiding unnecessary formality and seeking flexibility in the proceedings' and 'ensuring, so far as practicable, that the parties are able to participate fully in the proceedings'.

Rule 2 The Tribunal Procedure (First-tier Tribunal) (Social Entitlement Chamber) Rules 2008

Tribunals are courts of law. They are independent, they must apply the law and they must have a legally qualified judge. The tribunal asks questions, considers the evidence, establishes the facts and then applies the relevant law.

Although the tribunal is a court of law, it is different from most other courts, such as a criminal court. These have an 'adversarial' nature, where cross-examination may take place and one side may have to prove its case 'beyond reasonable doubt'.

A tribunal has a 'inquisitorial' role. It is more concerned with establishing the facts and considering the strengths and weaknesses of the evidence than with detailed legal arguments. The hearing is like a discussion or inquiry, rather than a conflict between two opposing sides, arguing 'for' and 'against'. The tribunal itself does most of the questioning, and there is no cross-examination. In rare cases where one side must prove its case, there is no requirement to prove it 'beyond reasonable doubt'. The test (called the 'burden of proof') is simply whether, on 'the balance of probability', it is more likely to be true than not.

A tribunal is therefore not as formal or potentially intimidating as a criminal or other adversarial court. The judge does not wear a wig or gown, there is no dock or witness stand and other lawyers are not usually present. Usually, oaths are not taken, although the tribunal may require this in some cases.

A tribunal's main objective is to deal with cases 'fairly and justly'.

There is more information about tribunal hearings in Chapter 6.

2. Do you have a representative?

What the law says

Representatives

A party to the appeal may appoint a representative (whether a legal representative or not) to represent her/him.

Once notified, a representative is assumed to be authorised to represent, and s/he must be sent any document which the person s/he is representing should be sent.

Parties to the appeal must help the tribunal to meet its overriding objective of dealing with cases fairly and justly, and generally co-operate with the tribunal.

Rules 2 and 11 The Tribunal Procedure (First-tier Tribunal) (Social Entitlement Chamber) Rules 2008

You and the 'decision maker' at the Department for Work and Pensions, HM Revenue and Customs or local authority are 'parties to the appeal'. As a party, you have a right to be represented by someone. A 'representative' does not have to be a lawyer. You do not have to have a representative, but it is strongly advisable, as s/he can help prepare your appeal.

Your representative's name and address should be notified to the tribunal. The tribunal can, if it wishes, still allow someone who has not been notified to represent. A representative has the same rights and responsibilities as a party to the appeal. In particular, this means s/he must help the tribunal to deal with the case and must co-operate with it.

Once you have notified the tribunal that you have a representative, s/he is assumed to be acting for you, unless you notify it in writing that this is no longer the case.

Your representative should be sent any documents about your appeal.

What is the representative's role?

There are not many rules about 'representatives' and their role. However, there is general agreement about what tribunals usually expect from a representative.

- S/he is not expected to be a legal expert. However, s/he is expected to know the case s/he wants to make, and ideally set this out in a written 'submission'. It is an advantage for her/him to know about the relevant law which is at issue in the appeal. Your representative is not just your companion.

- S/he should be able to say how the relevant facts and evidence support your case – eg, why the official medical report is inadequate or how the letter obtained from your GP is supportive. Tribunals often like this set out in a written submission.

- S/he is expected to have prepared you for the appeal hearing, so you know you will be questioned about the facts of your case – eg, about your illness and how it affects you.

- S/he should be polite and co-operative. Your representative is expected to assist the tribunal, not attack the 'other side', and aggressive conduct is disapproved of. However, s/he should still be assertive in pointing out the strengths of your case and the flaws in the decision that is being appealed.

At an 'oral hearing', the tribunal is unlikely to ask your representative many questions, as it wants to spend most of the time talking directly to you. The tribunal asks her/him to summarise the decision you are seeking and why. Your representative should be able to do this in a brief and concise way. Tribunals usually prefer this in a few sentences and bullet points in a written submission, ideally sent in advance of the hearing. **Note:** because the tribunal relies on your representative to state your case and the decision you want, this may mean that it does not consider things that your representative has not argued for (although it has the power to consider any aspect of the decision).

EXAMPLE

The decision being sought

Ben's appeal is about personal independence payment. His representative says that Ben does not dispute the decision concerning the 'daily living component', but wants to argue for the 'mobility component' to also be included. The tribunal decides not to consider the daily living component and to consider only the mobility component. Because the tribunal has the power to consider any aspect of the decision, it does not have to look at the daily living component.

The tribunal should know about the relevant law. So if your representative attempts to instruct the tribunal on the law, it may not be looked upon favourably. However, most tribunals do not object to representatives mentioning the law or caselaw if it is particularly relevant to your case. Knowing about the law relevant to the appeal is still important in most cases, as it helps your representative to understand what facts are relevant and what evidence you may need.

3. How do you prepare your appeal?

There is nothing in the law that says what you must or must not do to prepare your appeal. However, the following basic steps are likely to be the same in all appeals.

- Identify the 'point of the appeal'. What is your appeal about? What decision are you asking the tribunal to make?

- Check the law and caselaw that is relevant to the point of your appeal.

- Establish the relevant facts. If possible, gather further evidence that is relevant to the point of your appeal.

- Write a brief 'submission', setting out what you are asking the tribunal to do, and how the facts and evidence support your case.

- Ask for an 'oral hearing'. The tribunal can ask you questions at the hearing about the facts of your case. Ideally, your 'representative' should be at the hearing too.

Have you got a representative?

Your 'representative' can help prepare your appeal, including by gathering evidence, checking the law and writing a 'submission'.

If you cannot get a representative, you can still try to prepare your appeal, using the above basic steps. If doing all this is difficult for you, try to:

- get further evidence to support your appeal if you can – eg, a letter from your GP
- ask for an 'oral hearing' of your appeal and attend the hearing
- prepare to be questioned about the facts of your case

4. What is the point of the appeal?

The 'point of the appeal' is the basic matter of what your appeal is about – the decision you are unhappy with and what decision you are asking the tribunal to make in its place. In most cases, the point of your appeal is just about one or two things.

Knowing the point of your appeal as early as possible is vital so you can start to think about which facts and other information are relevant, and what evidence to get. Also, once you are clear about what the point of the appeal is, you can narrow down your search for the relevant law and caselaw.

The appeal papers sent to you before the hearing usually contain the history of your claim, claim forms, copies of decisions, as well as a 'submission' from the 'decision maker'. This is a statement of how the decision was made and what the tribunal may want to do.

EXAMPLES

The point of the appeal

John has been refused employment and support allowance because he has failed the 'work capability assessment'. He believes that more points should have been awarded to him in the mental health part of the assessment. In particular, John is asking for points for the activity concerned with coping with change. Whether points for this activity can be applied to John is the point of his appeal.

Angela has been refused housing benefit because her tenancy is said to be 'contrived' and not on a 'commercial basis', as her landlord is a friend and wanted to provide her with a home. However, Angela needed somewhere to live and there is an agreement to pay a reasonable rent to the landlord. So the point of Angela's appeal is her argument that the tenancy is not contrived and is on a commercial basis.

Anne has been told that she is not entitled to tax credits as a single person because she is living with Gareth as a couple. HM Revenue and Customs says it has information from a credit agency that Gareth has had bills sent to Anne's home address. However, Anne says that Gareth has not lived there for two years and, in any case, they were only ever friends, so they have never lived as a couple. The point of Anne's appeal is to show that she is a single person and is not living with someone as a couple.

Henri is French and has been refused universal credit because he is a European national and does not have a 'right to reside' in the UK. However, before falling ill, he worked part time and so had a right to reside as a 'worker'. The point of his appeal is that the decision maker was wrong to ignore this – had s/he taken into account the fact that Henri had been working, s/he would have decided that he kept his right to reside during a period of sickness.

This can often seem like a bewildering amount of information. However, try not to worry about the amount of information in the appeal papers. Once you have identified the point of your appeal, you will see that a lot of the information is only background material and, in fact, only certain parts of it are relevant to the point of your appeal.

Think of all the information in the appeal as being like a pyramid, with a lot of background information at the base, some partly relevant material in the middle, but most of the directly relevant material occupying just the top part of the pyramid. The top of the pyramid is the part that relates to the point of the appeal. If you concentrate on the material relevant to this, the mass of information will not seem intimidating.

How do you identify the point of your appeal?

Look carefully at why the decision you want to appeal makes you unhappy. Why is it wrong? If you have a 'representative', s/he should ask you about things that may have gone wrong – eg, if you think you had a poor-quality medical assessment, or if you did not include enough information on your claim form or questionnaire.

The point of your appeal may be clear from the decision. For example, if you have been refused employment and support allowance, the decision may state that it has been refused because you failed the 'work capability assessment' and include a list of the points that have been awarded (and not awarded) in the assessment.

More information about the appeal is in the appeal papers that are sent to you by the 'decision maker'. These include the decision being appealed, as well as copies of your claim forms, medical reports and the 'submission', including references to the law, from the decision maker. This information can help you identify the point of the appeal. However, as the appeal papers may not be issued until shortly before the appeal is heard, in practice, it is best to try and identify the point of the appeal before they are sent.

5. How do you check the law?

The tribunal knows about the law that is relevant to your appeal. The tribunal does not expect you to know about the law, and does not expect your 'representative', if you have one, to be a legal expert. However, it does expect your representative to know about the basic law that is relevant to your appeal. Most appeals do not involve complex legal issues.

When making its decision, the tribunal must apply the relevant law; it has no discretion to ignore or alter it. It is helpful to know about the relevant law to understand what the tribunal can and cannot do in your case.

What CPAG says

Checking the law

Social security law can sometimes be complex, and checking the law that is relevant to your appeal is an important part of preparation. However, many claimants have limited resources and have circumstances which make checking the law difficult. A good representative can check the law for you.

If you cannot get a representative, check the basic law yourself, using the advice in this chapter. This could also help you to think about the sort of facts and evidence that are relevant to your case.

What is social security law?

Social security law comprises two main things.

- **Legislation**, such as Acts of Parliament and regulations. This sets out the rules. Acts of Parliament set out the main rules in numbered sections. Regulations set out more detailed rules. These are numbered and may have sub-paragraphs.

- **Caselaw**. This clarifies how the rules in the legislation should be applied – eg, what the meaning of particular words or concepts in the regulations should be. The most common caselaw is in the form of decisions made by the 'Upper Tribunal'.

The 'First-tier Tribunal' must follow the decisions of the Upper Tribunal. If an Upper Tribunal decision is considered to be particularly important, it is 'reported'. If an unreported decision conflicts with a reported decision, the reported decision is normally applied.

A decision made by a three-judge panel of the Upper Tribunal is given preference to a decision made by a single judge.

In a few cases, caselaw is from the higher courts – the Court of Appeal, the Supreme Court (formerly the House of Lords), the Scottish Court of Session or the European Court of Justice. These take precedence over decisions of the Upper Tribunal.

Box A

Identifying an Upper Tribunal decision

Upper Tribunal decisions have reference numbers (called 'neutral citation numbers') in which the name of the claimant is abbreviated. Sometimes, the Secretary of State for Work and Pensions is also abbreviated. The Upper Tribunal and the name of the benefit are also abbreviated.

HB v SSWP (PIP) [2016] UKUT 160 (AAC) is the number of an Upper Tribunal decision about personal independence payment from 2016, in which the claimant's initials were HB and the decision maker whose decision was under appeal was the Secretary of State for Work and Pensions.

If the decision is 'reported', the number includes an additional reference at the end, which can be identified by the letter 'R' (for reported).

JS v SSWP (DLA) [2011] UKUT 216 (AAC); [2012] AACR 7 is the number of a reported Upper Tribunal decision about disability living allowance from 2011, in which the claimant's initials were JS and the decision maker whose decision was under appeal was the Secretary of State for Work and Pensions. The decision was the seventh case to be reported in 2012.

Decisions made by the old commissioners had different references. For example, CIB/14587/1996 was a decision of a commissioner (C) about incapacity benefit (IB) from 1996.

Before the Upper Tribunal was created, the judges who made the decisions were known as 'social security and child support commissioners' – usually shortened to 'social security commissioners'. These decisions are binding caselaw in the exactly the same way as Upper Tribunal decisions.

Decisions of the First-tier Tribunal are not caselaw: they do not have to be followed by 'decision makers' in other cases, or by other tribunals.

How do you find the relevant law for your appeal?

The relevant law is that which applies to the point of your appeal. It is not usually necessary to look up the law about things that are not closely linked to the point of the appeal – eg, when you have to make a claim, the fact that a particular test can be applied to your claim or when a decision on your claim can be made.

EXAMPLE

The relevant law

Niall appeals against a decision that he is not entitled to income-related employment and support allowance because he has failed the 'work capability assessment'.

His 'representative' identifies that the point of his appeal is whether Niall should score more points in the mental health part of the assessment and, if he does not score enough points, whether he should still be treated as passing the assessment because there would be a substantial risk to his health if this were not done.

The relevant law is where the work capability assessment, including the mental health assessment and the points that can apply, is set out. For income-related employment and support allowance, this is at Schedule 2 of the Employment and Support Allowance Regulations 2008. The rule about substantial risk is in regulation 29 of these regulations.

To find the relevant law, do the following.

- Firstly, look up a description of the relevant law – eg, use CPAG's *Welfare Benefits and Tax Credits Handbook* or Disability Rights UK's *Disability Rights Handbook*. If you have a representative, s/he may have a copy. Your local library may also have one.

- Next, look at the law itself. Legal references are in the endnotes of each chapter in CPAG's *Welfare Benefits and Tax Credits Handbook*.

- The law can be accessed online. The main official site is at http://lawvolumes.dwp.gov.uk. This is sometimes called the 'Blue Volumes'. Much legislation, including all new legislation, is at www.legislation.gov.uk.

- The law is accompanied by commentary in Sweet and Maxwell's *Social Security Legislation* books and in CPAG's *Housing Benefit and Council Tax Reduction Legislation*. The tribunal has copies of these books in the tribunal room, and usually places a lot of importance on what the commentary says. The commentary indicates the key decisions in the caselaw and describes the main points.

- Check for recent caselaw developments using the 'Upper Tribunal' website at www.justice.gov.uk/tribunals/aa (for the decisions themselves), the *Rightsnet* website (www.rightsnet.org.uk) and CPAG's *Welfare Rights Bulletin* (for descriptions of the decisions).

- Other organisations may have useful publications and websites. For example the *Adviser* magazine (published by Citizens Advice) summarises recent caselaw. The Disability Rights UK website (www.disabilityrightsuk.org) has information about benefits for people with illness or disability, including about benefit appeals.

EXAMPLE

Finding the relevant law

Lara's appeal is about her son Noah's entitlement to the 'care component' of disability living allowance.

1. Lara gets help from a representative at her local advice centre. Her representative identifies that the point of the appeal is to show that Noah needs frequent attention throughout the day and that the help he needs is substantially more than that needed by a child without a disability, so that he can get the middle rate of the disability living allowance care component.

2. Lara's representative uses CPAG's *Welfare Benefits and Tax Credits Handbook*. She looks up 'disability living allowance care component' in the index and then reads the description of the rules. This helps her to identify the issues.

3. Lara's representative then checks the notes at the end of the chapter for the relevant law. Using the abbreviations that are in an appendix at the end of the *Handbook*, she establishes that the basic rule is in section 72 of the Social Security Contributions and Benefits Act 1992.

4. Next, her representative looks up section 72 in Volume I of Sweet and Maxwell's *Social Security Legislation*. Here she can see the actual rule and also some commentary describing how relevant caselaw has interpreted it.

5. As a final check, Lara's representative looks at the Upper Tribunal website, the *Rightsnet* website and CPAG's *Welfare Rights Bulletin* for any recent caselaw that might be relevant.

Does your appeal have complex legal issues?

Usually, appeals do not involve complex legal issues. Most involve just one or two legal points that relate to the point of the appeal, and the tribunal is usually more concerned with facts, such as how your illness or disability affects you.

However, a few appeals do involve more complex legal issues – eg, if there is a question about whether a particular rule may be in breach of human rights legislation, or whether the law permits a particular regulation to have been made. Sometimes, the caselaw that has developed around a particular rule may be complex. Currently, the most common area of social security law that involves complex legal issues is the 'right to reside' test that applies to many benefits and to tax credits.

What CPAG says

Complex legal issues

If you are not experienced in social security appeals and there is a complex legal issue involved in your appeal, you should refer the case to a welfare rights adviser or 'representative', or at least get advice from such a person.

6. How do you gather facts and evidence?

Once you have checked the relevant law, you should gather the relevant facts and evidence. Exactly what facts and evidence are relevant depends on why you are appealing.

Box B
Facts and evidence: general tips

- Do not assume that the 'decision maker' already has all the relevant facts and evidence. For example, s/he may not have contacted your GP or consultant for further medical evidence.

- There may have been mistakes about some facts – eg, there may be an error in a medical report about how far you can walk. You should point these out to the tribunal – do not leave it to the tribunal to spot them. However, do not point out mistakes, such as simple spelling mistakes, just for the sake of it. Always consider whether it is relevant to the point of your appeal.

- Allow sufficient time to gather facts and evidence. It can be time consuming, but could be key to winning your appeal.

What are the relevant facts?

One of the main jobs of the tribunal is to establish the relevant facts. For example, if your appeal concerns your disability, relevant facts may include:

- how far you can walk
- how long it takes you to walk a certain distance or complete a certain kind of activity
- what kind of help you need with daily activities

If your appeal concerns whether you are living with another person as a couple, relevant facts may include:

- how you view your relationship with that person – are they just a friend?
- whether you share household duties
- whether you share bank accounts and bills

The tribunal expects you to help it establish the relevant facts as far as you can. You should point out any errors or things that have been left out to the tribunal. If you have a 'representative', s/he should make sure that you both understand what the relevant facts are in your case. In particular, check the following.

- What happened when you claimed? Did you represent your facts correctly on the claim form? If your appeal is about your illness or disability, do you think the doctor who examined you got all the correct facts?

- Claim forms and medical reports. Is there anything that is relevant, but which has been overlooked in the decision? Are there important mistakes in the medical report?

- The 'decision maker's' 'submission' in the appeal papers. Is there anything included that supports your appeal? Are there important mistakes?

EXAMPLE

Relevant facts

The point of Lucy's appeal is to show that she is entitled to the 'mobility component' of personal independence payment. The relevant facts are those about Lucy's ability to plan and follow a journey and to move around. Does she need help from another person when she is undertaking a journey? If so, what kind of help is this? How far can she walk? Can she walk without pain or breathlessness?

What evidence do you need?

What CPAG says

Evidence

Evidence (eg, from your GP) can be very important in winning your appeal. However, sometimes it is difficult to get such evidence – eg, if your GP refuses to supply it. You do not have an automatic right to be given further evidence for your appeal, and you may be charged for it. The tribunal does not get evidence for you, unless (in exceptional cases) it considers that is necessary for making a decision.

A good 'representative' may be able to help you gather facts and get further evidence – eg, s/he may be able to write to your GP or consultant to get a letter to help with your appeal. For more about this and difficulties in getting further medical evidence, see Chapter 5.

You are not automatically required to provide more evidence to support your appeal. What you say does not have to be supported by other evidence ('corroborated') to be accepted, and the tribunal can reconsider the decision on the basis of the evidence it already has.

However, in practice, most tribunals look for more evidence, and getting it will help your case. So, get supportive evidence if you can and, if possible, send it in to the tribunal in advance.

EXAMPLE

Relevant evidence

The point of Walid's appeal is to show that his tenancy is not 'contrived' and is on a commercial basis for housing benefit. The relevant evidence includes his tenancy agreement and his payment history. Why was the tenancy created? How much rent does he pay? Can Walid submit a copy of the tenancy agreement? Do his bank statements show regular amounts being paid to his landlord?

What evidence is important depends on what is at issue in your appeal. Bear in mind that the tribunal can consider any sort of evidence.

Box C
Evidence commonly used in appeals

- What you say at the 'oral hearing'. This is important evidence in a successful appeal. If you have a representative, the tribunal does not usually want her/him to give your evidence for you, unless you are unable to do so. However, your representative is allowed to ask you questions.

- A witness attending the oral hearing. This could be, for example, your carer or a relative, or even the person with whom you are alleged to be living with as a couple.

- Medical evidence, from your GP or consultant, district nurse or community psychiatric nurse. There is more information about medical evidence in Chapter 5.

- Evidence, such as a 'care diary', showing how the impact of your illness or disability varies over time. There is more information on this in Chapter 5.

- Non-medical information from a social worker or a carer, friend or relative can be helpful supporting evidence, showing how your illness or disability affects your daily life.

Can the tribunal ask you for further evidence?

What the law says

Tribunal directions about evidence

Tribunals can issue directions about the evidence they require, the way it is given and whether an oath is required. They can exclude evidence not provided as directed and can issue a summons to a witness.

Rules 15 and 16 The Tribunal Procedure (First-tier Tribunal) (Social Entitlement Chamber) Rules 2008

Although you are not automatically required to submit further evidence for your appeal, the tribunal can ask or 'direct' you to do so. However, in practice, this is uncommon. The tribunal is more likely to direct the 'decision maker' (ie, the Department for Work and Pensions, HM Revenue or Customs or local authority) to provide further evidence. You can ask the tribunal to do this if you think this is essential for the decision to be properly reconsidered.

EXAMPLE

Direction to provide medical reports

Monique is appealing against a decision that she fails the 'work capability assessment' and so is not entitled to employment and support allowance.

In the past, she has always passed the work capability assessment, and Monique feels she has not got any better since. However, the Department for Work and Pensions has not included the medical reports from all the assessments that she passed in the appeal papers. Monique asks the tribunal to direct the decision maker to supply these medical reports, because without them the decision about her failing the most recent assessment cannot be properly reconsidered.

How does the tribunal consider the evidence?

What the law says

Weighing evidence

Tribunals must give proper reasons for preferring one piece of evidence over another. 'Formulaic' reasons (eg, preferring the 'official' medical report) are not good enough.

Commissioner's decision CIB/3074/2003; Upper Tribunal decision AG v Secretary of State for Work and Pensions [2009] UKUT 127 (AAC)

The tribunal considers the evidence by 'weighing' it. This means it decides how much it can rely on each piece of evidence and whether (and to what extent) it should prefer one piece of evidence over another. It can discount some evidence entirely. For example, although what you say about your situation is evidence, a tribunal can discount it completely if it thinks what you say is improbable or contradictory, or it can prefer other evidence if it considers that is more reliable.

If you are disputing an official medical report, the tribunal may often give weight to medical evidence (eg, from a GP or consultant) submitted on your behalf. However, the tribunal should weigh the evidence according to its merits in your particular case, not assume that any one kind or source of evidence is always preferable. The tribunal should not assume that the official medical report is the best evidence available, just because it is the official report.

The tribunal should not assume that evidence is biased – eg, that your GP has supported you simply because you are her/his patient.

What the law says

GP's evidence

A GP is a professional person not forced by anyone to give one answer rather than another. S/he can say a claimant is exaggerating if s/he thinks this is the case.

Commissioner's decision CIB/14442/1996

Have your circumstances changed?

What the law says

Change of circumstances and evidence

The tribunal cannot take into account circumstances after the date of the decision under appeal, but can take into account evidence produced after that date, provided it is clear that it is about the circumstances that existed at the date of the decision under appeal.

Commissioner's decision R(DLA) 3/01

The tribunal can only consider the circumstances that applied on the date of the original decision. It cannot consider any change in your circumstances that occurs after this date, even if the change was before the 'mandatory reconsideration' of the original decision. So the evidence must be about your circumstances that applied at the time of the original decision. If the evidence is not clearly about those circumstances, the tribunal may decide to give it little 'weight'.

However, this does not mean that the evidence must have existed at the time. So, for example, a doctor's letter about your ability to walk should be about your ability to walk at the time of the decision being appealed – it does not matter if the doctor wrote the letter after this date.

7. How do you write a submission?

A 'submission' sets out your case, highlighting what you are asking for and how the relevant facts and evidence support this.

A written submission for your appeal is not strictly required, but it is a good idea to have one. It is usually written by your 'representative'. If you do not have a representative, the tribunal does not expect you to write your own submission. However, you can still do so. There is no particular submission form.

A submission does not have to be in writing – it could be stated verbally at the tribunal hearing. However, in practice, tribunals often find a written submission very helpful. If you have a representative, the tribunal will hope to get a submission from her/him.

Writing a submission and sending it to the tribunal is a good idea for the following reasons.

- It is a good way for you or your representative to set out your ideas for the appeal, and so it helps clarify your thinking.

- It means that you do not have to remember absolutely everything at the hearing – you can refer to the submission.

- If the submission is sent in advance, there is a chance that the 'decision maker' may change the decision in your favour without the need for a hearing.

- If the submission is sent in advance, the tribunal reads it before the hearing and it may help influence its thinking.

- Tribunals like written submissions. If you have a representative and s/he has sent a submission, the tribunal will think that s/he has been helpful and co-operative.

What should be in a submission?

There are no specific requirements for the content or layout of a 'submission'. Box D lists the basic principles that you should follow.

Box D
Basic principles for a submission

- Be brief. In most cases, a submission should be no more than a side or two of A4 paper.

- Set out the information clearly, with headings and numbered paragraphs.

- Identify the decision being appealed, and give your details and those of your 'representative'.

- At the start, include a summary of why you have made the appeal and what decision you would like.

- Set out the relevant facts and evidence. This need not be all the facts that have been gathered, just those relevant to the point of the appeal.

- Set out the reasons (known as 'representations') why your appeal should succeed – in particular, why the evidence shows that your appeal should be successful.

- At the end of the submission, briefly mention any law or caselaw that is especially important in your case. In many cases, there is nothing to point out, as the tribunal knows the basic rules that should apply. However, if you have identified some caselaw that is particularly relevant to the facts of your case, mention it. Refering to the caselaw commentary in the *Social Security Legislation* law volumes published by Sweet and Maxwell is also helpful – but always make sure that you or your representative read a full copy of any caselaw before it is used in a submission. Send a copy of the caselaw with your submission, in advance if possible.

- If a particular part of the decision is not being challenged, say so.

- You can make more than one argument. For example, if your appeal is about personal independence payment, you can ask that if the tribunal does not accept one 'descriptor' about your abilities, it consider an alternative one instead.

- Point out the strengths of your appeal – eg, where the evidence supports what you say. Do not leave it up to the tribunal to spot such things.

- Point out omissions or mistakes in the submission made by the 'decision maker', as well as in any official evidence, such as the official medical report.

- When pointing out things in the appeal papers, refer to the page number where they are located.

An example

You do not have to write a 'submission' in a particular way. If you have a 'representative', s/he may have developed her/his own preferred style and have a basic 'skeleton' submission which can be adapted to the facts of your case. However, the submission set out below is recommended as a basic structure and content.

EXAMPLE

Appeal submission

Rhian Evans is appealing against a decision, confirmed in a 'mandatory reconsideration notice', that she does not have 'limited capability for work' and so is not entitled to employment and support allowance. This is an example of a submission written by Rhian's representative. The representative has been able to get a supportive letter from the GP.

Submission

Claimant: Ms Rhian Evans [details of Rhian's address, telephone number and national insurance number]

Tribunal: [details of the tribunal reference number, hearing date and venue, if possible]

Representative: [name and work address of representative, including telephone number]

Date of decision under appeal: 3 November 2016

Date of mandatory reconsideration notice: 21 November 2016

1. Summary

Ms Evans appeals against the decision, dated 3 November 2016, that she does not have limited capability for work and is therefore not entitled to employment and support allowance. The decision was confirmed in a mandatory reconsideration notice, dated 21 November 2016.

She submits that she does have limited capability for work as she scores sufficient points in the work capability assessment.

Ms Evans submits that the following descriptors and points should apply, so that her points score is 18 and above the threshold.

- She cannot repeatedly mobilise 100 metres within a reasonable timescale because of significant discomfort or exhaustion (descriptor 1(c)(ii): nine points).

- She cannot cope with a minor planned change (such as a pre-arranged change to the routine time scheduled for a lunch break), to the extent that overall day-to-day life is made significantly more difficult (descriptor 14(b): nine points).

If the tribunal considers that descriptor 14(b) does not apply, it is invited to consider whether descriptor 14(c) (cannot cope with minor unplanned change: six points) applies instead.

If the tribunal is unable to find that Ms Evans scores sufficient points, please consider whether she should nevertheless be treated as having limited capability for work, on the basis that not to do so would pose a substantial risk to her health.

It is not submitted that Ms Evans satisfies the conditions for inclusion in the 'support group'.

2. Facts and evidence

2.1 Ms Evans suffers from a chronic back condition and depression, for which she is treated by her GP – see the letter from her GP, Dr Smith, on page 40 of the appeal papers. These conditions affect her daily life to a considerable extent.

Her back condition means:

- it is painful for her to bend and straighten up

- she has difficulty walking, to the extent that, although she may be able to walk 100 metres once, she could not do so again for a long time (three to four hours, and frequently longer) because of the pain that she experiences

2.2 Her ability to repeatedly mobilise seems not to have been considered in detail by the examining healthcare professional (pages 30–35). Ms Evans says that he seemed only to be concerned with her walking ability at its very best and did not ask about her ability to repeat this. Her GP confirms that she is likely to have this sort of problem with walking, and that she would be unable to propel herself in a manual wheelchair (page 40).

2.3 Ms Evans also experiences anxiety and depression, which is only moderately well controlled by medication (letter from Dr Smith, page 40). One of the effects of the depression is that she has great difficulty coping with minor changes to her daily routine, which tend to upset her to the extent that managing day-to-day life is much more difficult for her.

Ms Evans submits that this applies both to planned and unplanned changes in her daily routine. For example, she becomes greatly distressed by alterations to travel arrangments and her usual shopping routine. Ms Evans did state on her ESA50 questionnaire (page 35) that she often gets upset with such changes to her daily routine.

This is supported by her GP (page 40). Ms Evans says that the examining healthcare professional did not ask her many questions about this at the medical, and thinks therefore that he did not fully understand how the problem affects her.

3. Representations

3.1 This appeal is well supported by the evidence from Ms Evans and her GP, who has treated her for three years and knows her well. It is submitted that this should be preferred to the official medical report, as it is based on longer knowledge of her and a better understanding of her limitations. It is submitted that the official medical is partly inaccurate, as the examining healthcare professional did not properly explore the variability in Ms Evans's walking ability or the effects of her anxiety and depression.

3.2 The evidence shows that due to her inability to walk repeatedly and her inability to use a manual wheelchair, Ms

Evans satisfies descriptor 1(c)(ii). This descriptor scores nine points. This descriptor applies, because a person without restriction would be able to mobilise 100 metres several times a day.

3.3 Due to her anxiety and depression and, in particular, her inability to cope with minor changes, Ms Evans satisfies descriptor 14(b). This descriptor scores nine points. This descriptor applies, given the extent of distress caused to her by changes to everyday things like travel arrangements and shopping plans.

3.4 Alternatively, if the tribunal does not accept that descriptor 14(b) applies, it is submitted that, for the same reasons, descriptor 14(c) applies: inability to cope with minor unplanned change (six points).

3.5. If the tribunal is unable to find that Ms Evans scores sufficient points, it is submitted that she should be treated as having limited capability for work on the basis that there will be a substantial risk to her health if she is not. It is submitted that this arises from the risk that her anxiety and depression will be substantially worsened by having to cope with the demands of work, such as dealing with travel difficulties and even minor changes in her daily work routine.

4. Caselaw

No caselaw is submitted as especially relevant to this case.

Further information

Some basic resources for preparing for your appeal, including links to guidance, forms and caselaw, can be found on the CPAG website: www.cpag.org.uk/appeals-toolkit. If you are an adviser or representative and your client's appeal involves complex legal issues, you can contact CPAG's advice service for further help. This is not for people dealing with their own benefits claim – get help first from an adviser or representative at a local advice centre. See www.cpag.org.uk/advisers if you are an adviser in England and Wales and www.cpag.org.uk/content/advice-line-frontline-advisers-and-support-staff-scotland if you are in Scotland.

Chapter 5
Appeals about illness and disability

This chapter covers:

1. What problems may arise?

2. Medical evidence

3. What can the tribunal do?

4. How can you increase your chances of winning your appeal?

What you need to know

- Appeals about illness and disability are similar to other appeals. However, particular problems sometimes arise.

- Medical evidence is often important in these appeals, but there can be problems getting this and using it at the tribunal.

- The tribunal cannot take into account any changes in your circumstances that occur after you have appealed, including if your condition has got worse.

- The tribunal can use evidence from another of your benefit claims. It can also decide to make a decision that is less favourable to you than the one you appealed against.

1. What problems may arise?

Many appeals are about illness or disability. In particular, many appeals are about the 'work capability assessment', used to decide whether you qualify for employment and support allowance or an additional amount in universal credit, and the disability tests used for personal independence payment and disability living allowance.

Box A
The work capability assessment

The work capability assessment is the test used to decide whether you have 'limited capability for work' – ie, whether you are currently unable to work. The test is used to decide your entitlement to employment and support allowance, and also whether you get an additional amount in your universal credit because you or your partner are ill or disabled. The assessment normally involves your completing a questionnaire and attending a medical examination.

In addition, the work capability assessment tests whether you have 'limited capability for work-related activity'. This is to identify whether your illness or disability is so serious that you should not be expected to plan returning to work. If you are assessed as having limited capability for work-related activity, you get the 'support component' of employment and support allowance, and can get the 'limited capability for work-related activity' element in your universal credit.

If your appeal is about your illness or disability, the main rules about the way the tribunal deals with your appeal are the same as for any other appeal. However, problems sometimes arise, including the following.

- Getting medical evidence. Your doctor may refuse to supply further evidence or want to charge for supplying it.

- Considering medical evidence. The tribunal may automatically prefer the official medical report, or give the medical evidence from your doctor little 'weight'.

- The tribunal cannot take into account any changes in your circumstances while you are waiting for your appeal to be heard, even if your condition gets worse.

- The tribunal may want to make a decision that is less favourable to you than the one you appealed against.

2. Medical evidence

You are not automatically required to get further medical evidence for your appeal. However, in practice, it is best to obtain additional medical evidence if you can, as it may increase your chances of winning your appeal.

What CPAG says

Getting further evidence

Although the tribunal has knowledge of medical matters and disability, it does not conduct a medical examination (unless your appeal is about industrial injuries disablement benefit). The appeal papers usually contain the official medical report so, unless you provide further evidence, there can sometimes seem to be an imbalance in the evidence that is available to the tribunal. Although further medical evidence is not essential to win your appeal, it is often important.

Your 'representative' may be able to help you get further medical evidence – eg, by writing to your doctor.

Further medical evidence is often a supportive letter from a doctor – eg, a GP or consultant. You can also get supportive medical evidence from:

- an occupational therapist
- a physiotherapist
- a clinical psychologist
- a community psychiatric nurse
- existing medical evidence – eg, a previous medical report (ESA85), when you passed the 'work capability assessment'

Sometimes, evidence from people who are not medically qualified may also be relevant – eg:

- social workers
- support workers
- care workers

Has your doctor refused to provide medical evidence?

Your doctor is under no obligation to provide you with medical evidence for your appeal. Doctors must supply information to the 'decision maker' if they are requested to do so, but not to you or your 'representative'.

In practice, workload and other pressures (including information from the Department for Work and Pensions emphasising that they do not have to supply evidence to claimants) has led to an increasing number of doctors, especially GPs, refusing to supply medical evidence.

If your doctor refuses to supply evidence to you, you can:

- try to persuade her/him to provide the evidence (see Box B)
- find other medical evidence to support your appeal (see Box C)

Box B
Persuading your doctor to provide evidence

- Make sure your doctor knows that the very point of an appeal is because something may have gone wrong with the official medical assessment and that the tribunal must consider the accuracy of the official medical report.

- Emphasise that you only need a short letter, not a lengthy medical report.

- Point out that your doctor may have much better knowledge of you than the health professional who carried out the official medical, who has only examined you once.

- Ensure that your doctor knows that many appeals are successful.

- If your doctor does supply supportive evidence, remember to thank her/him and let her/him know the outcome of your appeal.

If your doctor cannot be persuaded to supply further medical evidence, other medical evidence may already exist. Some of this may be in the appeal papers – eg, the official medical report may say some things in your favour.

> Box C
> **Finding other medical evidence**
>
> - Ask your doctor for a copy of your GP records that are held electronically. You may be charged for this.
>
> - Is there medical evidence in the appeal papers that supports your appeal – eg, a copy of a previous medical report in which you passed the 'work capability assessment'?
>
> - Is your appeal about the work capability assessment? If so, if there is a previous medical report (ESA85) that is still relevant because your condition has not changed but which is not in the appeal papers, the Department for Work and Pensions can be told ('directed') by the tribunal to include it, as otherwise the hearing may not be fair.
>
> - Is there a medical report produced for another benefit that you have claimed that may be relevant? In particular, medical reports from personal independence payment or disability living allowance claims may be used as evidence in employment and support allowance appeals, and vice versa. They must be relevant and used with care, bearing in mind that the benefits have different rules.
>
> - Do you have an occupational therapy assessment or a social worker's report that may be helpful?
>
> - The tribunal could get further medical evidence to use in your appeal, if it considers that this is necessary for its decision. However, it is rare for a tribunal to do this as it usually already has the medical evidence. If it does get further medical evidence, this is not necessarily from your doctor – it could be from the Department for Work and Pensions. You are not charged for this.

Alternatively, medical evidence may have been produced about another matter that is relevant to your appeal. This evidence is not usually as useful for your appeal as a letter from your doctor, but it may still be helpful.

What the law says

Previous medical reports

A tribunal is not always obliged to consider previous medical reports. However, it should do so where relevant, or where a claimant says there has been no change in her/his medical condition or disablement and that the evidence is relevant.

Upper Tribunal decision FN v SSWP [2015] UKUT 670 (AAC)

Is there a charge?

Your doctor may be willing to provide you with further medical evidence, but may wish to charge you for it. There is no rule preventing this, or limiting the amount that your doctor can charge. You may pay the charge if you are able and willing to do so. It is unlikely that your 'representative' will be able to pay for you.

If you cannot afford to pay, consider the following.

- Emphasise to your doctor that you have been refused benefit and cannot afford to pay.

- Make it clear that your representative is unable to pay.

- Emphasise that you only need a short letter, not a lengthy medical report.

- In Scotland, legal aid may be able to pay for the evidence, if you are eligible. Your representative may be able to help you apply.

What CPAG says

Charging for medical evidence

Your representative could consider liaising with your GP and other local doctors, by, for example, arranging a meeting at a local medical centre, to explain the importance of their support with appeals. This could be done in collaboration with people working on appeals in other organisations. In response to such liaison, some GPs have reduced their charges, or dropped them altogether.

How do you ask for medical evidence?

To be given 'weight' by the tribunal, your medical evidence should focus on what is relevant to your appeal. For example, a diagnosis and list of treatments is less useful than a letter stating how you are affected by your condition, ideally referring to the point of the appeal. However, it is best to make it clear that you are asking the doctor to express her/his own opinion. You should not attempt to pressurise her/him into giving the evidence you want.

- Ask for a short letter focusing on the point of the appeal, rather than more general information.

- Ask 'open' questions, asking for the doctor's own view, rather than 'closed' or leading questions simply asking the doctor to agree with what you say, or giving her/him the answer that you want. An example of an open question is: 'The tribunal will be considering whether the following statements can be applied. Can you comment?' An example of a closed or leading question is: 'Can you confirm that I cannot walk more than 20 metres?'

- Ask for brief reasons for the opinion s/he gives. If the evidence is in the form of an opinion only, it may be given less weight.

- Ensure the evidence relates to your abilities at the time of the original decision being appealed. The tribunal cannot take into account any changes since that date, even if the change was before the date of the 'mandatory reconsideration' of the decision. It does not matter if the evidence itself is produced at a later date.

- If your 'representative' is requesting the evidence for you, s/he must have written authority from you giving your permission for the doctor to supply the evidence.

- When sending medical evidence to the tribunal, include your letter asking for the evidence, so that the tribunal can see what you said to the doctor.

EXAMPLE

Letter requesting medical evidence

This letter is from a representative who is helping Rhian Evans with her appeal.

Dear Dr Smith,

Re: Rhian Evans, 12 Bevan Road, Splott, Cardiff

Date of birth: 3/3/70

We are writing on behalf of the above who we understand is your patient. We include a form of authority from her.

Following a medical assessment on behalf of the Department for Work and Pensions, Ms Evans has been refused employment and support allowance, as she is not considered to have limited capability for work. She has, with our assistance, appealed against this decision to an independent tribunal. The tribunal will reconsider the decision, and has the power to uphold it or decide that it should be changed. We are writing on behalf of Ms Evans to ask if you could provide a short letter to assist with that.

We appreciate that your time is limited. However, the tribunal will find a short letter focused on the relevant questions more helpful than a longer medical report.

The tribunal will be considering whether the following statements, taken from the official work capability assessment, may be applied to Ms Evans on the date of the decision (3 November 2016). The tribunal cannot take into account any changes in her condition after that date.

We would be grateful if you could comment on whether you agree or disagree that these statements may be applied to Ms Evans, with a brief indication of your reasons, or are instead unable to comment. A brief statement of any medication and treatment she has would also be helpful.

1. Cannot repeatedly mobilise (including using a walking stick, manual wheelchair or other aid which is normally, or could normally be, used) 100 metres within a reasonable timescale because of significant discomfort or exhaustion.

2. Cannot cope with a minor planned change (such as a pre-arranged change to the routine time scheduled for a lunch break), to the extent that overall day-to-day life is made significantly more difficult.

Please be advised that as Ms Evans is on a very low income and our organisation has very limited funds, neither she nor ourselves can meet a charge for supplying the letter. If you do propose to charge, please contact us before proceeding.

Thanking you in advance for your assistance.

Yours sincerely [etc]

How does the tribunal consider the medical evidence?

There are very few rules on how a tribunal should consider ('weigh') medical evidence. It should make up its own mind about what should apply. It should consider each piece of evidence on its own merits, without assuming that one sort of evidence is automatically better than another. For example, a very short piece of evidence from a doctor that is general in nature may be given less weight by the tribunal than a detailed medical report that focuses specifically on the issues. Chapter 4 has more information about general principles that apply when weighing evidence.

Weighing medical evidence

The official medical report should not automatically be preferred to the claimant's own evidence.

Upper Tribunal decision MW v SSWP [2016] UKUT 76 (AAC)

Holding that the official medical report must automatically be preferred to that of the claimant would fly in the face of the obligation of the tribunal to consider all the evidence.

Commissioner's decision R(DLA) 3/99

In incapacity and disability cases, the appeal is, in effect, against the official medical report, and to say that it is automatically to be preferred is not the correct approach.

Commissioner's decision CIB/3074/2003

The tribunal may prefer the evidence of a GP who has treated the claimant over many years; in others it may prefer the evidence of a specialist who is skilled in the condition from which the claimant suffers. It may attach little weight to a 'terse' certificate from a GP.

Commissioner's decision R(M) 1/93

Tribunals should not give 'formulaic' reasons for endorsing the official medical report – ie, merely on the basis that it is 'expert' and by someone trained in applying the test.

Upper Tribunal decision AG v Secretary of State for Work and Pensions [2009] UKUT 127 (AAC)

A GP is a professional person not forced by anyone to give one answer rather than another. The tribunal should not assume that the claimant is putting words in the GP's mouth.

Commissioners' decisions CIB/14442/1996 and CDLA/2277/2005

The GP's letter included express views and the tribunal should not have implied that the doctor had merely acted as a 'cipher' for what the claimant said.

Upper Tribunal decision HL v Secretary of State for Work and Pensions (DLA) [2011] UKUT 183 (AAC)

In the past, some tribunals have wanted to give more weight to an official medical report automatically, simply because it is the official medical report. Problems have also arisen when tribunals have taken a critical attitude to the medical evidence produced for claimants – eg, by saying that doctors have been asked 'leading' questions or are biased in favour of their patients.

Generally, such approaches are wrong in law. The tribunal should not assume that the official medical report is automatically correct and should not make any assumptions – eg, that your doctor is acting under pressure from you. For the tribunal to be justified in deciding that your doctor is acting under pressure from you, it must give specific reasons based on the facts of your case.

If you think the tribunal's approach is incorrect, ask for clarification of why it is taking it. If necessary, refer to supportive caselaw. **Note:** if a tribunal bases its decision on an incorrect approach, this may be an 'error of law', which could be challenged in a further appeal to the 'Upper Tribunal'.

3. What can the tribunal do?

Can the tribunal take a change in your condition into account?

A tribunal cannot take into account a change in your circumstances, including a change in the condition of your health, that occurs after the date of the original decision that is being appealed. This applies even if your circumstances changed after this date, but before the date of the 'mandatory reconsideration' of the decision.

If your condition changes while you are waiting for your appeal to be heard, there are two main consequences for winning your appeal.

- Any evidence produced for your appeal should refer to your condition on the date of the original decision. If this is not possible, it may be possible to argue that it does not matter – eg, if your medical condition has been the same for some time and is clearly not likely to vary much over time. Remember that it is only a change of *circumstances* that cannot be taken into account by the tribunal. It can still take into account evidence produced after the decision.

- Any significant change in your health condition after the date of the decision being appealed cannot affect the outcome of the appeal, as the tribunal cannot take it into account. This applies even if your condition gets much worse while you are waiting for your appeal to be heard. In practice, this is is common, as it can take several weeks or months before appeals are heard.

What should you do if your circumstances change?

If your health condition changes while you are waiting for your appeal to be heard, get advice about how this affects your benefit entitlement. Depending on the facts of your case, the situation could be complex.

If you are getting benefit, you have a duty to report any change in your circumstances that you might reasonably be expected to know might affect your benefit award. So if your condition improves in a way that might affect your benefit entitlement, you must report this.

If your condition gets worse while you are waiting for your appeal to be heard, you could do one of the following.

- Report the change in your circumstances. This will lead to another decision being made on your benefit entitlement.

- Wait for the tribunal to make its decision and then report the change. However, you might miss out on some arrears of benefit.

- Report the change in your circumstances, but ask the 'decision maker' not to make a decision until the tribunal has decided your appeal.

The more serious the worsening in your condition, the greater the case for reporting it. Remember the following general points.

- In an appeal about 'limited capability for work', if you report a change in your circumstances, this may lead to the 'work capability assessment' being carried out again. Your appeal against the original decision still goes ahead, whatever the outcome of that assessment. However, if you also fail the second work capability assessment, the decision maker may stop your entitlement continuing, even if your appeal is successful. In this case, you must then make another appeal against the decision about the second failed work capability assessment.

- On the other hand, if you have a second work capability assessment and you pass, any increase in your benefit entitlement can start straight away, with the tribunal considering only the period between the original decision and the start of entitlement from the second work capability assessment.

- If you are appealing a decision to refuse you personal independence payment or disability living allowance and your condition gets worse, you could make a new claim while your appeal is pending. If you were awarded some benefit (eg, at a lower rate than you asked for), you can ask for this to be looked at again. In either case, you usually get a new (a second) decision and the tribunal then considers just the period between your first and second decisions. If you are also unhappy with the second decision, you must make another appeal against that.

Can the tribunal use evidence from another benefit claim?

What the law says

Evidence about another benefit

A tribunal can consider medical evidence from an appeal about another benefit, but should do so carefully and bear in mind that different legal tests are involved.

Upper Tribunal decisions LD v Secretary of State for Work and Pensions [2009] UKUT 208 (AAC) and DK v Secretary of State for Work and Pensions (DLA) [2012] UKUT 254

Because a tribunal can take into account any evidence that is relevant, it can sometimes take into account evidence from another benefit claim or appeal. This is most likely if the appeal papers contain such evidence.

You may have two appeals at the same time – eg, you may be appealing about the 'work capability assessment' for employment and support allowance and the way your disability has been assessed for personal independence payment. In this situation, your appeals are considered at separate sessions and by differently comprised tribunals. Ideally, you and your 'representative' should attend both hearings.

Although your appeals are heard separately, evidence from one appeal can be used in the other – eg, if your appeal concerns your disability and how it affects you, some issues (such as your ability to walk) may be common to both appeals. The tribunal should ensure that you and the 'decision maker' can see this evidence and are able to comment on it. As the tribunals are separate, it is possible that they might take different approaches and arrive at different conclusions.

EXAMPLE

Using evidence from another benefit claim

Saoirse's appeal is about a decision that she failed the work capability assessment for employment and support allowance, and includes whether she should score more points for her problems with walking. She has also claimed personal independence payment and been awarded the standard rate of the 'mobility component' because of the difficulty she has walking. The tribunal can take any relevant evidence from the personal independence claim, including about her walking, when deciding her employment and support allowance appeal, even though the tests for walking ability for the two benefits are different.

Box D

Appealing about more than one benefit: tactics

- Consider whether any evidence from your other appeal is useful – eg, is it a potential source of supportive medical evidence? If so, what are its strengths and why should the tribunal give 'weight' to it? If you want the evidence from your other appeal to be considered, you should submit it to the tribunal.

- Are there weaknesses in the evidence from the other appeal? Do you think that the medical examination in the other claim was of poor quality for some reason?

- Remember that the different appeals concern different legal tests and, if necessary, emphasise that to the tribunal.

Can the tribunal make a less favourable decision?

The tribunal can completely reconsider the decision being appealed and can also make whatever decision the 'decision maker' could have made. It can therefore make a decision that is less favourable to you than the one you appealed against.

This is the case, even if you have not specifically appealed against all parts of the original decision. The tribunal does not have to look at the aspects that you do not want changed, but it can if it thinks they may be wrong. If it is going to do this, the tribunal should warn you and, depending on the facts of your case, give you a chance for an adjournment of the hearing to get advice or more evidence, or to consider withdrawing your appeal.

Making a less favourable decision is most likely in some personal independence payment and disability living allowance appeals. This is because there are a number of things that concern your entitlement in the decision: whether you are entitled to one or both 'components', the rate you get and for how long. So an appeal about one aspect of the decision allows the other aspects to be considered too.

EXAMPLE

A less favourable decision

Jalal receives a decision that he is entitled to the 'daily living component' of personal independence payment at the standard rate, but that he is not entitled to the 'mobility component'. Jalal thinks he should get the mobility component too and so appeals.

However, after considering the evidence, the tribunal thinks that it may refuse his appeal about the mobility component, and also alter the original decision to remove his entitlement to the daily living component.

The tribunal warns Jalal that it is considering this. If he decides to continue with the appeal, the tribunal has the power to take away the daily living component as well as to refuse the mobility component. If this happens, Jalal will lose all his personal independence payment.

In appeals about the 'work capability assessment', it is less common for a tribunal to make a less favourable decision. However, the tribunal could, for example, reduce the total points score awarded to you, or even decide that you do not pass the assessment at all, even though you have only appealed against the decision not to place you in the 'support group'.

If you have appealed against a decision that you fail the work capability assessment and the tribunal agrees with you and decides that you do in fact pass it, it should also consider whether you should be in the support group, as this is also part of the decision being appealed.

Box E
Avoiding a less favourable decision

- Is there an element of the decision on your claim that is at risk of a less favourable decision? For example, have you been awarded a personal independence payment component that you are happy with (and so have not appealed about), but which might not be very secure?

- If so, consider whether it is advisable to continue with the appeal. Remember, the tribunal can look at all elements of the decision.

- If the tribunal indicates that it wishes to consider a part of the decision that you do not want changed, it should let you know and allow you at least a brief adjournment. It may offer you the opportunity of a longer adjournment to consider the unappealed part of the decision, or allow you to withdraw your appeal. If you have a representative, the tribunal expects her/him to help you decide what to do.

- Be careful about declining an offer of an adjournment. If you do this but then later wish to argue that the tribunal should have granted one, it will be very difficult to succeed.

- If you want to get further evidence about the unappealed part of the decision, or want more time to consider the evidence about this, the tribunal should allow an adjournment, but it is not obliged to.

4. How do you increase your chances of winning your appeal?

In many ways, appeals about illness or disability are no different from any other appeal. So, in order to maximise your chances of success, do the following.

- Have an 'oral hearing' of the appeal, attended by you and, ideally, your 'representative'.

- Provide evidence that supports your appeal, such as a letter from your GP or consultant.

There are other things that you can do to increase your chances of winning an appeal about the 'work capability assessment' or an appeal about your disability.

Work capability assessment appeals: is there a risk to health?

What the law says

The substantial risk rule

If you do not score sufficient points in the work capability assessment to win your appeal, you should still do so if there would otherwise be a substantial risk to your physical or mental health, or to someone else's physical or mental health, unless that risk could be avoided by reasonable adjustments.

Regulations 29 and 35 The Employment and Support Allowance Regulations 2008; Schedule 8 paragraph 4 and Schedule 9 paragraph 4 The Universal Credit Regulations 2013; regulations 25 and 31 The Employment and Support Allowance Regulations 2013

If you are appealing against the outcome of the 'work capability assessment' that decides whether you have 'limited capability for work' for benefit purposes, you can increase your chances of success by understanding a particular rule that is sometimes overlooked. This treats you as satisfying the assessment if there would be a substantial risk to your (or to someone else's) health if you were found not to have limited capability for work.

The rule applies to the assessment of your limited capability for work and your 'limited capability for work-related activity'.

Check whether you can argue that there is a substantial risk, even if you are also arguing about the number of points that should be awarded to you in the assessment. You can argue that you should score enough points and that a substantial risk applies if you do not score enough points. The substantial risk could be from doing the sort of work or work-related activity that you may be expected to do.

The tribunal does not need to consider actual job descriptions, just the kind of work that you might be able to do. Risks can arise from travelling to or from work.

What the law says

Substantial risk

In a case about limited capability for work, the tribunal should, when considering substantial risk, assess the range or type of work which a claimant is capable of performing in assessing the risk to her/himself or to others. That can include the journey to or from work.

Court of Appeal decision Charlton v Secretary of State for Work and Pensions [2009] EWCA Civ 42; commissioner's decision R(IB) 2/09; Upper Tribunal decision IM v SSWP (ESA) [2014] UKUT 412 (AAC); [2015] AACR 10

If your appeal is about whether you have limited capability for work-related activity, the tribunal should have evidence about the kind of work-related activity in your area that the Department for Work and Pensions considers you could do without incurring substantial risk.

EXAMPLE

Substantial risk

Eva appeals against a decision that she fails the work capability assessment and so is not entitled to employment and support allowance. She experiences anxiety and depression, and has problems coping with change and with social situations. In the past, her mental health problems have been severe and she has harmed herself.

The tribunal decides that Eva does have limited capability for work and therefore satisfies the work capability assessment, and so allows her appeal. Although the tribunal did not score her sufficient points to pass the assessment, it decided that if she did not pass the assessment, the pressures of a working environment would pose a substantial risk to her health. Her mental health would be affected and this may cause her to harm herself again.

Disability appeals: keeping a diary

If you are appealing about personal independence payment, disability living allowance or attendance allowance, a care or mobility 'diary' can be a helpful source of additional evidence, especially if there are significant fluctuations in your condition, so that you tend to have good and bad periods.

The disability test for personal independence payment requires that a particular 'descriptor' (a statement describing your ability to carry out a number of activities) must apply for more than 50 per cent of the days in the one-year period taken into account when deciding your entitlement. There is no specific rule for disability living allowance and attendance allowance, but the test looks at whether you satisfy the disability test for 'most of the time'.

A diary, in which you record the level and frequency of your care needs or your walking ability over a period of time, can therefore help show whether you satisfy the test. When recording your walking ability, try to indicate not only how far you can walk, but also other relevant things such as whether you are using an aid (eg, a walking stick or frame), how long it takes you to walk as far as you do, and whether you need to stop because of discomfort or breathlessness.

You do not need to keep your diary in any particular form, but be as clear and as accurate as possible – eg, use a page for each day. Ideally, keep your diary over a period of time that most accurately reflects fluctuations in your condition. So, if you tend to have good days and bad days, a period of a few weeks is probably enough; but if you tend to have good weeks and bad weeks, you may need to keep it for a month or more.

Further information

An example of a care diary to help with a claim for disability living allowance for a child is in Disability Rights UK's *Disability Rights Handbook*.
CPAG's *Personal Independence Payment: what you need to know* outlines the assessment criteria used for personal independence payment, including the activities you are tested against and the points you must score to qualify for an award.

Chapter 6
The appeal hearing

This chapter covers:

1. What happens before the hearing?

2. What happens at the hearing?

3. What happens after the tribunal has made its decision?

What you need to know

- Your appeal is considered either at an 'oral hearing' or by the tribunal looking at the appeal papers. You are more likely to win your appeal if you attend an oral hearing.

- Your appeal can be cancelled ('struck out') if you do not respond to queries from the tribunal clerk.

- Oral hearings can be 'postponed' or 'adjourned', but there is no legal right to this.

- There are no precise rules about how hearings are run, but there is an overall requirement to be fair.

- Most tribunals give their decision on the same day as the hearing. Some decisions may be given later in writing.

1. What happens before the hearing?

After you have made your appeal, it may be some time before it is heard by the tribunal.

What happens after you appeal?

Most benefits and tax credits

For most benefits (except housing benefit) and tax credits, you can only appeal after a 'mandatory reconsideration'. You then send your appeal directly to HM Courts and Tribunals Service.

When HM Courts and Tribunals Service receives your appeal, it checks to make sure it is valid. If it thinks there are any problems that need to be rectified, it returns the appeal for you to correct. For example, it may ask you to add your reasons for the appeal. Do not ignore this request. If you do, there is a risk that the appeal will be cancelled ('struck out').

If your appeal is considered valid, or if HM Courts and Tribunals Service thinks that any problems can be ignored (or 'waived'), it sends an acknowledgement of this to you. This includes the contact details and telephone number of the office handling your appeal. It may also include an enquiry form if it needs more details about your availability or requirements for the appeal, such as whether you want an 'oral hearing', details of your 'representative' and whether you need an interpreter.

A copy of your appeal is sent to the 'decision maker' at the Department for Work and Pensions or Her Majesty's Revenue and Customs. S/he prepares a 'response' to the appeal, explaining how the decision was made. The decision maker must do this within 28 days.

The decision maker's response is sent as a 'bundle' of appeal papers to the HM Courts and Tribunals Service and to you. If you have notified that you have a representative, s/he should be sent the appeal papers. However, check with her/him, as this sometimes does not happen. The decision maker's response must include:

- the decision that is being appealed
- copies of the relevant documents, such as claim forms and official medical reports
- a 'submission' to the tribunal, including a summary of the relevant facts and the decision maker's reasons for making the decision
- a copy of the appeal form or letter

You or your representative can send further documents and make a written submission as a reply to the decision maker's response. At least a month should be allowed for this.

If you think that the decision maker has not included information or evidence which is relevant to your appeal (eg, an official medical report, which in the past resulted in your being awarded the benefit you are now appealing about), you can ask the tribunal to 'direct' the decision maker to supply it.

Housing benefit

Appeals about housing benefit can be made directly against the original decision, so a mandatory reconsideration is not required. Send your appeal to the decision maker at the local authority.

The decision maker prepares a response to the appeal and sends this to HM Courts and Tribunals Service and to you. S/he must do this 'as soon as reasonably practicable'. The decision maker's response must include:

- the decision that is being appealed
- copies of the relevant documents, such as claim forms and official medical reports
- a submission to the tribunal, including a summary of the relevant facts and the decision maker's reasons for making the decision
- a copy of the appeal form or letter

HM Courts and Tribunals Service then takes over the handling of your appeal. It sends you an enquiry form asking about your availability, whether you want an oral hearing, details of your representative and other matters.

Is there a delay by the decision maker?

In the past, there have sometimes been long delays in 'decision makers' referring appeals to HM Courts and Tribunals Service or in responding to appeals.

If there is a delay by the decision maker, you can ask HM Courts and Tribunals Service to contact her/him and require that action be taken.

The tribunal can issue a 'direction' to the decision maker requiring her/him to provide documents, information or evidence, or it can set a date for the hearing. The tribunal is more likely to issue a direction if you can show that the delay is causing you particular problems – eg, because of your reduced income, you are at risk of homelessness or the interests of a child or another vulnerable person are being adversely affected.

Does HM Revenue and Customs want to settle your tax credit appeal?

If you have appealed against a tax credit decision, HM Revenue and Customs may want to 'settle' it before it is considered by the tribunal. This can only happen if you consent.

If the appeal is settled, it 'lapses' – ie, it does not go ahead. So think carefully about whether or not to agree.

If you agree to settle, the terms of the agreement must be sent to you in a written notice. The appeal then lapses unless you write back within 30 days of the date of the written notice saying that you have changed your mind and want the appeal to go ahead.

If the appeal is not settled, HM Revenue and Customs prepares its response and sends it in the appeal papers to HM Courts and Tribunals Service and to you. HM Courts and Tribunals Service then takes over the handling of the appeal in the usual way.

Can the appeal lapse?

Once you have appealed, the 'decision maker' can still change the decision before the appeal is heard. If s/he does this and the new decision is more advantageous to you (even if it still does not give you everything you want), your appeal 'lapses' (ie, it does not go ahead), unless you renew it.

If you are contacted about this, ask your 'representative' for advice. Unless the new decision gives you everything you have asked for in your appeal, it is usually better to say that you still want to appeal.

If a new decision is issued before the appeal is heard, and you do not want your appeal to lapse, make sure you renew your appeal.

It is not very common for an appeal to lapse.

Types of hearing

HM Courts and Tribunals Service normally arranges for an 'oral hearing' of your appeal to take place. This is usually a face-to-face hearing that you and, ideally, your 'representative' attend. The other 'parties to the appeal', such as the Department for Work and Pensions or the local authority, can also attend the hearing.

Having an oral hearing is strongly advisable: you are much more likely to win your appeal if there is one. Only at an oral hearing can the tribunal ask you questions and find out more about your situation – eg, what happened at your medical examination. It is possible for there to be an oral hearing which your representative attends, but you do not. However, this is not advisable, as the main value of an oral hearing is that the tribunal can ask you questions.

Your appeal is dealt with at an oral hearing unless all the parties to the appeal agree to its being dealt with using the case papers and the tribunal agrees it can decide the case in this way. You are sent a form asking whether or not you want an oral hearing.

In exceptional cases (eg, if you want to attend the hearing but this will never be possible because of your health or disability), the tribunal can conduct an oral hearing which you attend by telephone or video link, rather than face-to-face. Request such a hearing if you need one. However, these are discretionary and, in practice, are rare.

If there are exceptional circumstances, an oral hearing can also take place in your home. This is called a **'domiciliary hearing'**. This can be arranged if HM Courts and Tribunals Service accepts that you cannot get to a tribunal venue because of a severe disability. If you request a domiciliary hearing, you should send a letter from a doctor confirming that you are unable to travel, including by taxi. Your request may not be accepted.

If there is no oral hearing, the tribunal considers the 'submissions' and the evidence in the appeal papers – this is known as considering the appeal **'on the papers'**.

Although you do not have the stress of attending an oral hearing, remember that the chances of winning your appeal are significantly lower with a paper hearing.

The tribunal clerk contacts you (or your representative) to arrange a date for the hearing and to inform you of where the hearing will be held. The clerk may allow you more time to gather evidence or get a representative, but does not have to. Be as clear as you can about why you need a later date and when that could be.

What happens if you cannot attend the hearing?

If a hearing date has been set and this is not suitable for either you or your 'representative', contact the tribunal clerk as soon as possible, explain your situation and request an alternative date. Put your request in writing and well in advance, although you can ask again on the day of the hearing if necessary.

If you have said that you will attend an oral hearing but at the last minute find that you cannot or that you will be late, let the tribunal clerk know as soon as possible.

What happens if your representative cannot attend the hearing?

Your 'representative' should do as much as s/he reasonably can to be available for an 'oral hearing' if s/he wishes to attend. Before it considers an alternative date, the tribunal expects her/him to have a good reason why s/he cannot attend and why there is no alternative representative available – eg, it may expect her/his advice centre to arrange for another representative to attend. If a particular date is not suitable, s/he should explain as soon as possible why this is the case, including, for example, why another representative cannot be there.

If your representative becomes unavailable at the last minute, you can request for the hearing to be 'postponed' – but the tribunal is not legally obliged to do so.

Box A
Attending an appeal without your representative

- Make sure your representative has prepared a written 'submission' and sent this to the tribunal in advance. This is particularly important, as it is the only statement by your representative of your case. It should state clearly that a representative will not be attending the hearing, but that you will.

- The submission should point out any particular difficulties you are likely to encounter during the course of the hearing – eg, because of nervousness or embarrassment.

- Ask your representative for a copy of the submission to take to the hearing.

- You can be accompanied by someone, such as a friend or a relative, for general support and reassurance. However, make it clear to the tribunal that this person is not acting as your representative.

- Discuss your case with your representative before the hearing, so that you are prepared for the questions the tribunal may ask you.

- Make an appointment with your representative for after the hearing, to discuss what happened. Your representative can take notes in case they may be of use if you appeal further to the 'Upper Tribunal'.

In general, the appeal can proceed without your representative, especially if there is no explanation about why s/he cannot attend. However, the tribunal must still ensure that you get a fair hearing, and it should take your desire to be represented seriously. So if your representative is unavailable, the tribunal may postpone the hearing. If a postponement is needed on the day of the hearing, this is called an 'adjournment'. The tribunal does not have to do this: it depends on the facts of your case.

If your representative cannot attend a hearing (eg, because of limited resources in the advice centre), s/he can still do all the work involved in preparing your appeal, including sending a written submission to the tribunal on your behalf.

Even if your representative cannot attend the hearing, you should still attend so the tribunal can ask you questions.

Can the hearing be postponed or adjourned?

What the law says

Postponements and adjournments

The First-tier Tribunal may adjourn or postpone a hearing. If a party fails to attend a hearing, the tribunal may proceed in her/his absence if the tribunal is satisfied s/he has been notified of the hearing and considers that it is in the interests of justice to proceed.

Rules 5 and 31 The Tribunal Procedure (First-tier Tribunal) (Social Entitlement Chamber) Rules 2008

Once a date has been set for the hearing of your appeal, before the day of the hearing it can be 'postponed' (ie, put off) until a later date. Once a hearing has started, it can be 'adjourned' (ie, paused) until another day.

The tribunal does not have to postpone or adjourn the hearing, and usually does not do so unless it is absolutely necessary. If you apply for a postponement or adjournment, explain your reasons for your request as fully as possible.

Whether or not a hearing is postponed or adjourned depends on the facts of your case. The tribunal should bear in mind the need to deal with all cases 'fairly and justly', and should be prepared to consider your request. It must also deal with cases flexibly. 'Parties to the appeal' are expected to co-operate with the running of the appeal, including making sure, as much as they can, that their case is ready. In general, a tribunal may adjourn for something like a sudden illness, but not if you or your 'representative' repeatedly ask for more time to produce evidence.

What the law says

Adjourning an appeal

If an adjournment has been requested, the tribunal is likely to focus on the following questions: What would be the benefit of an adjournment? Why was the party not ready to proceed? What impact would an adjournment have on the other party and on the operation of the tribunal system?

Upper Tribunal decision MA v Secretary of State for Work and Pensions [2009] UKUT 211 (AAC)

In practice, a tribunal is often happy to grant a very short adjournment (such as for 10 minutes or so to enable you or your representative to collect your thoughts), but is reluctant to adjourn until another day. However, it may do so if you have new evidence or arguments on the day of the hearing, which it thinks the other party to the appeal must be given time to consider.

If a postponement or adjournment is refused, the hearing goes ahead, and you and your representative must be prepared to continue. If a postponement is refused, you can still request an adjournment on the day of the hearing. If refused, the hearing takes place.

Can you withdraw your appeal?

If you withdraw your appeal, it is not considered by the tribunal, and the original decision that you appealed against stands.

You can withdraw your appeal in writing at any time before the tribunal starts the hearing. You do not have to give any reasons.

Once the tribunal has started the hearing, or if your hearing has been adjourned and the tribunal has directed that you need its permission to withdraw your appeal, the appeal can only be withdrawn with the tribunal's consent. In this case, you may have to give your reasons.

If your appeal has been withdrawn, it can be reinstated by the tribunal. For this to happen, you (or the Department for Work and Pensions, Her Majesty's Revenue and Customs or the local authority) must apply to the tribunal in writing. Your application must be received within one month of the date the tribunal received your application to withdraw.

Can your appeal be cancelled?

An appeal can be cancelled (known as being 'struck out') by the tribunal in the following circumstances.

- You have not complied with a tribunal 'direction' – eg, you have not supplied information it has requested. Your appeal is cancelled automatically if the direction stated that a failure to comply would lead to your appeal being struck out. Make sure that you always respond promptly.

- The tribunal does not have jurisdiction to deal with the appeal – eg, because there is no right of appeal against the decision.

- The tribunal considers that your appeal has no realistic prospect of success.

- You have failed to co-operate with the tribunal to the extent that the case cannot be dealt with 'fairly or justly'.

If your appeal is cancelled because you have not complied with a direction from the tribunal, you can apply for the appeal to be reinstated. You must do so in writing, and your application must be received within a month of the date of the the letter telling you that your appeal has been struck out, although longer may be allowed. Your application should be accompanied by your reasons – eg, about why you could not reasonably comply with the direction.

In other situations, it is not possible to reinstate your appeal. However, before your appeal is cancelled, you must first be given a chance to comment and say why the appeal should not be struck out – eg, why you had a good reason for not co-operating with the tribunal.

If your appeal has been struck out and/or the tribunal refuses to reinstate it, you can appeal further to the 'Upper Tribunal'.

How do you prepare for the hearing?

You should discuss your case with your 'representative' before the hearing. You should both be clear about what you consider to be the relevant facts, and what your case will be.

Be prepared for the tribunal to ask you questions about the relevant facts in your case. This is the most important part of the 'oral hearing'. The questions will depend on what your appeal is about and the facts of your case. Being prepared for questioning does not mean that you should give prepared answers or behave in a particular way. You should respond to the tribunal's questions as honestly and as accurately as you can. Try not to exaggerate or to underestimate things when giving your answers, and be as clear as you can.

You will not be asked questions about the law, but your representative may be asked whether s/he has relied on a particular rule or piece of caselaw.

More information about how you are questioned, and the kind of questions you are asked, is on pages 107–08.

Will the tribunal question a child, a vulnerable adult or sensitive witness?
Tribunals often decide not to question a child, even if s/he is the benefit claimant – eg, if s/he is getting disability living allowance. However, the tribunal should take account of the child's age, maturity and wish to take part in the proceedings and balance this with the need to take into account her/his welfare.

Tell the tribunal in advance if you do not want your child to be at the hearing and be questioned – eg, because s/he is very young or too ill.

What the law says

Questioning children, vulnerable adults and sensitive witnesses

The tribunal only asks a child, vulnerable adult or sensitive witness questions if it considers it necessary for a fair hearing and that the person's welfare will not be 'prejudiced'. In deciding what to do, the tribunal should consider all the available evidence and, for example, what the child's parent or carer (or representative) says.

The tribunal should take account of a child's age, maturity and wishes if s/he is participating in a hearing about her/his own appeal. **Note:** this Upper Tribunal decision modifies the above.

First-tier and Upper Tribunal Practice Direction, 'Child, Vulnerable Adult and Sensitive Witnesses', 30 October 2008; Upper Tribunal decision JP v SSWP (DLA) [2014] UKUT 275 (AAC)

The tribunal does not usually question a vulnerable adult or sensitive witness and will not if her/his welfare would be harmed. In some circumstances, if it is appropriate, it should consider whether to question her/him by telephone or video link.

If your appeal involves a vulnerable witness (this could be you – eg, if you are very ill or disabled) and you have a representative, it is helpful for your representative to alert the tribunal in advance to some of the things it should bear in mind when asking questions and considering answers.

Checklist: before the hearing

Box B
Final preparations for the hearing

- Check that you or your 'representative' have your appeal papers and a copy of your 'submission' to take to the hearing.

- Remember that the tribunal will ask you questions.

- Plan to arrive in good time at the tribunal venue.

- You are not required to dress formally at the hearing, although your representative may wish, for example, to wear a suit. Ensure that you feel comfortable.

Box C
Checklist for representatives

- Check that both of you are familiar with the submission. It will damage your client's chances of winning her/his appeal if you say different things at the hearing.

- Ensure that your submission has been sent to the tribunal in advance, with any further evidence and any letters asking for such evidence. Take spare copies of these documents to the hearing. Remember that if you hand in your submission on the day, this may cause an adjournment.

- Think about the sort of questions the tribunal may ask your client and ensure s/he understands that you cannot usually answer for her/him.

- Make any witnesses aware of what the tribunal will be like and the sort of questions they may be asked.

- Take the appeal papers and copies of any legislation that is particularly relevant.

- Do not forget to take writing materials to make notes.

2. What happens at the hearing?

'Oral tribunal hearings' take place on the date, and at the time and place, notified (unless there has been a 'postponement'). Some appeals may be held on Saturdays.

What the law says

Tribunal hearings

The tribunal may 'regulate its own procedure' and 'give a direction in relation to the conduct or disposal of proceedings at any time'.

Rule 5 The Tribunal Procedure (First-tier Tribunal) (Social Entitlement Chamber) Rules 2008

There are no set rules on exactly how a tribunal hearing must be run or the order in which things must happen. Instead, there are rules that give the tribunal wide discretion to decide what happens. The main requirement is that the hearing be fair – that everyone is given a chance to put their case, and that there is no bias.

The judge usually decides exactly what happens and in what order. This includes deciding, if necessary, that part of the hearing should be in private. It also includes giving a 'direction' to a 'party to the appeal' – eg, to produce a particular piece of evidence. For instance, the Department for Work and Pensions can be directed to produce a medical report.

A typical hearing is as follows.

- The judge introduces the tribunal. The parties to the appeal may be invited to outline their case.

- The tribunal asks questions. Most of the questions are to you – ie, the person who has made the appeal.

- Closing statements are taken, and the tribunal considers its decision.

What happens when you arrive?

When you arrive at the tribunal venue, you wait in a waiting room. You are met by the tribunal clerk, who asks whether you have any expenses for attending the appeal, such as travel expenses or loss of earnings. Your 'representative' cannot claim expenses. The clerk also asks whether you have any further evidence that you want to submit, and whether you have any witnesses.

If you do not have a representative, the clerk may give you a brief outline of what is likely to happen in the hearing. If you have any questions about this, ask her/him.

Depending on the venue, there may be other people in the waiting room. Usually, these will be other claimants and their representatives, as the tribunal hears a number of cases each day. Someone from the Department for Work and Pensions, HM Revenue and Customs or local authority (known as the 'presenting officer') may also be in the waiting room.

When the tribunal is ready to start, the clerk asks all the 'parties to the appeal' (you, your representative and the presenting officer) into the tribunal room. If there is a witness, s/he may be asked to wait outside the tribunal room until the tribunal is ready to ask her/him questions.

Who is the presenting officer?

Sometimes, there may be someone from the body (eg, the Department for Work and Pensions) that made the decision you are appealing. This person is called a 'presenting officer' and is there to explain the decision.

A presenting officer is a 'party' to the appeal and can make 'submissions' and ask questions. Her/his role is supposed to be a 'friend of the court', to help the tribunal make its decision, not to defend the decision under appeal at all costs. The presenting officer may be in the waiting room or in a waiting room of her/his own. S/he should not be in the tribunal room until the hearing starts.

The presenting officer can ask you questions, although this is not common. S/he should not attempt to cross-examine you as if you were a witness or a defendant in a criminal trial – s/he should ask questions to help the tribunal make its decision.

In recent years, it has become increasingly common for presenting officers not to attend hearings.

What is the tribunal room like?

Tribunal rooms may differ slightly from venue to venue. In most cases, the tribunal members are seated on one side of a large table. They usually sit on normal chairs, not on a raised platform. The judge sits in the middle, with the other members of the tribunal (if present) alongside.

The tribunal has copies of the appeal papers and the legislation, including the *Social Security Legislation* volumes, published by Sweet and Maxwell. The tribunal clerk is there to assist with other information and administrative matters.

The 'parties to the appeal' and their 'representatives' are invited to sit on the other side of the table. You are usually asked to sit in the middle (opposite the judge), with your representative to one side and the 'presenting officer' to the other. The clerk sits on an adjoining side of the table, but often leaves and re-enters the room during the course of the hearing. The clerk may be working at a computer during the hearing.

Who are the members of the tribunal?

Tribunals comprise one, two or three members, depending on the type of decision being appealed. There is more information on this in Chapter 2.

The tribunal members do not wear judicial wigs or gowns. They are, however, likely to be dressed relatively formally, wearing suits or other smart dress. They usually refer to themselves (and can be addressed) as 'Mr', 'Mrs' or 'Ms', although there are no rules about such things. Some judges refer to themselves as 'judge'.

Who else may be present?

Usually, there is no one else present at the tribunal apart from the members of the tribunal, the 'parties to the appeal' (you, your 'representative' and, if present, the 'presenting officer') and the clerk.

Sometimes, someone undergoing training with HM Courts and Tribunals Service may be present to observe the hearing. S/he sits to the side or at the back of the room.

Witnesses may be present if they have been called by one of the parties to the appeal or under a 'direction' from the tribunal. In many appeals there are no witnesses. If there are witnesses, the tribunal usually directs that they are only in the room when it is their turn to be questioned.

In theory, hearings are heard in public and any member of the public can attend. In practice, this rarely happens. If you want to protect your privacy, you can ask the tribunal to exclude members of the public.

How does the hearing begin?

First, the judge introduces the tribunal panel to you. If your hearing is being recorded, s/he explains this and asks everyone present (except the clerk) to introduce themselves for the recording.

The judge explains what the tribunal is and what its job is. S/he usually emphasises its independence.

Usually, the judge summarises what is at issue in the appeal and may invite the 'parties' to outline their case, although s/he could move straight on to the evidence and questions.

This means that early in the proceedings the judge may ask your 'representative' to outline the decision you are seeking, or whether there is anything to add to your written 'submission'.

During the hearing, the judge makes notes. If your hearing is not recorded, these notes are what is known as the 'record of proceedings'. If your hearing is recorded, the recording is the record of proceedings. This is not part of the decision, but can be requested after the hearing.

How are you questioned?

Usually, after the case has been outlined, the tribunal begins by asking questions. The judge and the other members of the panel may all ask you questions.

The main aim of the questioning is to get oral evidence from you. This usually means that you are questioned about factual matters relevant to your appeal and the facts of your case.

For example, in a disability appeal you may be asked how far you can walk, whether you can concentrate on reading a magazine or watching a television programme, or about what happened at your medical examination. In an appeal about whether you are living with another person as a couple, you will probably be asked about the nature of your relationship with that person, and whether you share household duties and pool your finances. In an appeal about an 'overpayment', you may be asked about what you told the benefits office about your circumstances, income and capital, and what happened afterwards. In appeals about the 'work capability assessment', personal independence payment and disability living allowance, one of the members of the tribunal is medically qualified and is likely to ask questions about your treatment and medication.

The tribunal usually tries to be friendly, but can sometimes seem abrupt. You may be asked some sensitive or embarrassing questions (eg, about your medical condition and how it affects your daily life), but this is often necessary in order to get the evidence required. The tribunal does not want your 'representative' to answer for you. It may ask your representative some questions about your written 'submission', but often says relatively little to her/him.

If you become upset or confused by the questioning, indicate this to the judge and ask whether it is possible to slow down, or rephrase the questions. Your representative can ask for this on your behalf. If you become very upset, the tribunal may allow a short 'adjournment'.

In an exceptional case, the tribunal may allow your representative to speak for you.

At some point in the hearing, the tribunal usually asks the 'parties to the appeal' if they want to ask any questions. The judge decides when this happens. Your representative may want to ask you some questions in order to clarify a point that s/he thinks is important and has perhaps been misunderstood or ignored. The 'presenting officer' may also ask questions.

The tribunal also questions any witnesses attending the hearing. For example, if a relative or carer has accompanied you to the hearing to give evidence about the sort of help you need at home, the tribunal asks her/him questions about this. Usually, the witnesses are asked to wait outside the tribunal room until the tribunal is ready to ask them questions, and to leave the tribunal room when the questioning is finished.

EXAMPLES

Questioning

Sofia's representative thinks that Sofia has been confused by the questions the tribunal has asked, and asks the judge if she can put a question to Sofia. The judge agrees, although he asks her representative to wait until the tribunal has finished asking questions.

Maggie becomes upset during the hearing. Her representative indicates this to the judge and respectfully asks if the tribunal could put the questions in another way.

Fred's representative wants to give a lot of details about Fred's appeal at the start of the hearing. The judge asks the representative just to outline the basis of the appeal, and explains that the tribunal will ask Fred some questions. The representative is given a chance to put his own questions to Fred, and make any other comments, before the hearing ends.

Is there a medical examination?

The tribunal does not conduct a medical examination, except in industrial injuries disablement benefit cases. In an industrial injuries disablement benefit appeal, there is usually a pause in the proceedings and you are taken into an examination room to be examined by the medical member of the tribunal. In any other appeal, the tribunal is not permitted to examine you physically – so it cannot, for instance, ask you to remove an item of clothing.

However, the tribunal can observe your behaviour, such as your walking ability when you enter the tribunal room or your ability to remain comfortable throughout the hearing, and use those observations as evidence.

How does the hearing end?

When all the evidence has been heard by the tribunal, the judge usually asks whether there are any 'closing statements'. This is your or your 'representative's' chance to briefly sum up the case, drawing attention to particular strong points and emphasising any particular points that have come up during the hearing. If your representative wants to ask you any questions in order to clarify something or emphasise a particular point, the tribunal may allow him/her to do so.

The 'parties to the appeal' and their representatives are then asked to leave the tribunal room while the panel makes its decision.

In most cases, the tribunal makes its decision and gives this to you on the day, although it is not required to do so. If the judge thinks that a decision cannot be made on the same day and needs to be sent in writing later, s/he will say so.

When the tribunal has made its decision, you are invited back into the tribunal room to be informed. Sometimes, the tribunal may invite only your representative back, as tribunals often prefer to deal with the representative at this stage. However, if you wish to be present, this should normally be allowed.

The decision notice

The decision is given verbally by the judge, along with a short written summary, called the 'decision notice'. This is the formal end to the hearing. It is not a further opportunity to make points or ask questions.

When you have left the tribunal room after getting the decision notice, make sure that you understand the decision. Check this with your representative if necessary.

Sometimes, the tribunal posts the decision notice to you at a later date.

The decision notice should tell you that you can request a 'statement of reasons' for the decision, and include the conditions for making a further appeal to the 'Upper Tribunal'. There is more information about this in Chapter 7. If a 'presenting officer' was at the hearing, s/he normally makes sure that the organisation that made the original decision (eg, the Department for Work and Pensions) gets the decision notice. If not, the clerk sends it.

3. What happens after the tribunal has made its decision?

Did you win your appeal?

If you win your appeal, usually the decision refusing you benefit is replaced with one awarding you benefit.

Although the tribunal decision is binding, the 'decision maker' is responsible for implementing it, not the tribunal. Sometimes, the decision maker may need to make further decisions about your entitlement – eg, if the tribunal has decided that you have a 'right to reside' for benefit purposes, the decision maker then needs to assess your income and capital. The tribunal has no legal power to enforce payment.

The decision maker can ask for a 'statement of reasons' for the tribunal's decision. This must normally be done within one month. There is more information on a statement of reasons in Chapter 7.

In rare cases, the decision maker may want to appeal to the 'Upper Tribunal' against the tribunal's decision. If this happens, payment of your benefit following the appeal is suspended. However, a further appeal is only considered when an important legal principle is at issue. In the majority of cases, the decision maker does not appeal further.

Can you be paid arrears?

If you win your appeal, you may be entitled to arrears of benefit that was not paid while the appeal was pending.

Sometimes, arrears are reduced by the amount of another, 'overlapping' benefit that was paid to you while you were waiting for the appeal to be decided. An overlapping benefit is one that cannot be paid at the same time as another. For example, if you were paid jobseeker's allowance while waiting for your appeal about employment and support allowance to be decided, the two benefits will have overlapped and the arrears of your employment and support allowance are reduced by the amount of jobseeker's allowance you received. In general, arrears of personal independence payment and disability living allowance are not reduced.

Box D
Q&A: winning an appeal

Q: Lenka's appeal was about the 'work capability assessment'. Does winning mean that she will always have 'limited capability for work'?

A: No. The Department for Work and Pensions can still arrange further medicals to assess her limited capability for work in the future. The tribunal may have recommended how long it should be before she is reassessed, but the Department for Work and Pensions does not have to follow this. The same applies to decisions about the tests for personal independence payment and disability living allowance.

Box E
Q&A: winning an appeal

Q: Archie wins his appeal. When will he start getting his money?

A: There is no set period. In most cases, benefit starts to be paid again within a few weeks of the tribunal's decision. If there is a delay, contact the decision maker and ask for payment to begin as soon as possible.

Did you lose your appeal?

If lose your appeal, you have a number of options. Ask your 'representative' or an advice centre about what to do next.

- Consider whether the decision could be 'set aside' (this means it is cancelled and your appeal is heard again) or whether you can make a further appeal to the 'Upper Tribunal'. There is more information about this in Chapter 7.

- If the tribunal awarded you some benefit, but not everything you asked for, and your circumstances have changed since the tribunal decision, consider asking the 'decision maker' to look at the decision again and make a new decision on your entitlement. A decision that changes a decision made by the tribunal is called a 'supersession'. **Note:** even if the supersession increases your benefit award, you are only paid from the date you applied for the supersession.

- Accept the decision and if possible reclaim benefit (eg, if you now qualify because your circumstances have changed) or make a claim for a different benefit.

Box F

Q&A: losing an appeal

Q: Sasha was paid employment and support allowance while waiting for her appeal to be decided. Does she have to pay this back, now that she has lost her appeal?

A: No. The decision maker only removes your entitlement from the date of the tribunal's decision, so Sasha remains entitled to the employment and support allowance that she was paid – although her award now stops.

Q: Teresa lost her appeal about failing the 'work capability assessment'. Can she try to claim employment and support allowance again?

A: Yes. However, she will not be paid again straight away, unless she has a new condition, or her condition has significantly worsened and the decision maker thinks it is now likely that she will pass the assessment.

Q: Sean lost his appeal about entitlement to personal independence payment. Can he reapply?

A: Yes, although any entitlement he may now have only starts from the date of his new claim. In practice, the decision maker may look to see whether there has been any change of circumstances that means s/he should not make the same decision as was made previously. But there is nothing to prevent a repeat claim.

Q: Liam lost his appeal about being entitled to tax credits as a single person because it was decided he was part of a couple. This means he has been overpaid. Can he appeal if HM Revenue and Customs decides to recover the overpayment?

A: No. A decision to recover an overpayment of tax credits cannot be appealed, although this decision can be disputed with HM Revenue and Customs. If he would have been entitled to tax credits as part of a couple, he should ask for the overpayment to be reduced by the amount he would have got.

Chapter 7
After the appeal

This chapter covers:

1. Are you unhappy with the tribunal's decision?

2. Can the tribunal decision be changed?

3. Can you make a further appeal?

4. Appealing to the Upper Tribunal

What you need to know

- A summary of the tribunal's decision is usually given to you on the day of the hearing.

- You can request a 'statement of reasons' for the tribunal's decision. You should do this particularly if you lost your appeal and want to appeal further.

- A tribunal decison can be changed if there has been an accidental mistake or by being 'set aside' – ie, it is cancelled and reconsidered.

- You can make a further appeal to the 'Upper Tribunal' if there was an 'error of law' in the tribunal decision, but not simply because you disagree with it.

1. Are you unhappy with the tribunal's decision?

If you lost your appeal and you are unhappy with the decision, you may be able to get the decision changed or make a further appeal.

Getting the decision changed can be done relatively quickly, but there are very limited situations ('grounds') when this can be done. If the decision contains an 'error of law', you can make a further appeal to the 'Upper Tribunal'. In practice, in order to show that there is an error of law in the tribunal's decision, you will usually need a 'statement of reasons' for the tribunal's decision.

How are you notified about the decision?

A short written summary of the tribunal's decision (the 'decision notice') is usually given to you on the day of the hearing. Sometimes, the tribunal posts the decision notice to you at a later date.

The decision notice should tell you that you can request a 'statement of reasons' for the decision, and include the conditions for making a further appeal to the 'Upper Tribunal'.

The statement of reasons

What the law says

Statements of reasons

A written statement of reasons must be supplied, if requested, within one month of the date on which the decision was given.

Rules 33 and 34 The Tribunal Procedure (First-tier Tribunal) (Social Entitlement Chamber) Rules 2008

The 'statement of reasons' is longer than the 'decision notice'. It includes what the tribunal has decided are the facts of your case (known as the 'findings of fact') – eg, what the tribunal thinks are the relevant facts about your health condition and how this affects you). It also includes a full explanation of why the tribunal made its decision. For example, it should explain the evidence the tribunal preferred (if any) and why it preferred it. Sometimes, the statement of reasons may be referred to as the 'full written decision' or 'written reasons'.

It is important to have a statement of reasons if you want to appeal further to the 'Upper Tribunal'. This is because there must be an 'error of law' in the decision in order to appeal to the Upper Tribunal and it is often difficult to show that there is an error of law if there is no statement of reasons.

Sometimes, the tribunal provides a written statement of reasons for its decision automatically. If not, you can request one from the tribunal.

You must ask for a statement of reasons in writing. If your request is received by the tribunal within one month of the decision notice being given (or sent), it must provide one. If your request is outside the one-month time limit, the tribunal can still provide one, but does not have to. If your request is late, explain why.

The tribunal should send you a statement of reasons within a month of your request 'or as soon as is reasonably practicable' after that period.

The time limit for appealing to the Upper Tribunal does not start until the statement of reasons is sent. If there is a long delay, contact HM Courts and Tribunals Service and ask what the reason for the delay is, and for the statement of reasons to be sent as soon as possible.

The record of proceedings

The 'record of proceedings' may comprise the judge's written notes or, if your hearing was recorded, the recording. It is not a formal part of the tribunal's decision. It is not usually sent to you as a matter of course, even if you request a 'statement of reasons'.

If you want to appeal against a tribunal decision, it is not essential to have a record of proceedings. However, it is sometimes a good idea to request one at the same time as requesting a statement of reasons, as it can provide more background to the decision and help identify any 'errors of law'.

You must apply for a record of the proceedings in writing within six months of the date of the tribunal's decision. The tribunal may still supply one if your request is made outside this time limit, but does not have to, and records of proceedings may be destroyed after six months. The tribunal is not obliged by law to provide a record of proceedings, but if you have requested one within the time limit and it refuses, this might indicate that its decision might not be as well founded as it should be.

2. Can the tribunal decision be changed?

The tribunal decision can be changed if certain conditions are met. Unless it is changed, the decision is binding.

What the law says

Clerical mistakes and set asides

The tribunal may at any time correct any clerical mistake or other accidental slips or omissions in a decision.

The tribunal may set aside a decision which disposes of proceedings and remake the decision.

Rules 36 and 37 The Tribunal Procedure (First-tier Tribunal) (Social Entitlement Chamber) Rules 2008

If you want the tribunal decision to be changed, you should get advice from your 'representative' or an advice centre.

Any 'party to the appeal' can try to change a tribunal decision in one of the following ways.

- A clerical mistake or another accidental slip or omission can be corrected by the tribunal itself. This is to allow decisions to be altered quickly if there has been a simple error or 'slip of the pen'.

- In certain circumstances, the decision can be cancelled (called being 'set aside') and the appeal heard again.

- If there is an 'error of law' in the tribunal decision, it can be appealed further to the 'Upper Tribunal'. If you apply for a further appeal and there is a clear error of law, the tribunal can review its own decision before it is reconsidered by the Upper Tribunal, in which case you should be notified of your right to appeal against this. **Note:** the 'decision maker' usually only tries to appeal further if the decision involves a general point of legal principle.

- If the decision includes an award of benefit, it can be looked at again by the decision maker if there are grounds to do so. This is called a 'supersession' if it is about a benefit or a 'revision' if it is about tax credits. Usually, this happens if there has been a relevant change in your circumstances since the date of the decision – eg, if your medical condition changed while you were waiting for your appeal to be heard. A supersession cannot be carried out just because the decision maker thinks the decision is legally wrong. In this case, s/he must try to appeal to the Upper Tribunal.

When can the decision be cancelled?

A tribunal decision can only be cancelled ('set aside') in certain circumstances. The main purpose is to allow a decision to be cancelled quickly if something went wrong with the tribunal procedure. Whether or not a decision can be set aside depends on the facts of your case.

The tribunal sets a decision aside if it considers that it is 'in the interests of justice' to do so and:

- a 'party to the appeal' or her/his 'representative' did not receive the appeal papers or other relevant documents in sufficient time for the hearing
- a party to the appeal was not present at the 'oral hearing' (except if s/he had chosen not to attend)
- there was some other 'procedural irregularity'

In addition, the tribunal's decision *must* be set aside if either you or the 'decision maker' apply for a further appeal to the 'Upper Tribunal' and both you and the decision maker agree that the decision contains an 'error of law'. However, this circumstance very rarely arises.

You must apply for a decision to be set aside in writing. This must be received by HM Courts and Tribunals Service no later than one month after the date on which the tribunal decision was sent. In practice, as you are usually told the decision on the day of the hearing, this will be within one month of the date of the hearing. The tribunal can allow longer, but it does not have to. If your request is late, explain why.

When you ask for a decision to be set aside, you can also ask that if your request is refused, you be sent a 'statement of reasons' (because you may then want to consider whether there are grounds for a further appeal to the Upper Tribunal).

If the decision is set aside, the appeal must be heard again and a new decision made. If the decision is not set aside, the tribunal can treat your application as an application for permission to appeal to the Upper Tribunal or as an application to correct the decision.

If the tribunal refuses to set aside the decision, you may be able to appeal against this decision to the Upper Tribunal, as sometimes the reason for a set aside may also be an error of law. For example, if relevant evidence was not included in the appeal papers, this is potentially both a ground for the decision to be set aside and an error of law because it breached the rules of natural justice. If this applies to you, it may be worth trying to appeal to the Upper Tribunal about both the refusal to set aside and against the tribunal decision itself.

3. Can you make a further appeal?

Note: this guide only covers some very basic rules on further appeals. If you want to appeal further, you should speak to an experienced adviser.

What the law says

Appealing to the Upper Tribunal

There is a right of appeal to the Upper Tribunal on any point of law arising from a decision made by the First-tier Tribunal, other than an excluded decision.

Section 11 Tribunals, Courts and Enforcement Act 2007

If there is an 'error of law' in the 'First-tier Tribunal's' decision, you can appeal further to a different tribunal, called the 'Upper Tribunal'. All 'parties to the appeal' have the right of further appeal. **Note:** if you do not have a 'statement of reasons', it may be difficult to show whether there has been an error of law.

You can appeal against most tribunal decisions, including not only the final decision of the tribunal but also decisions about matters like a refusal to accept a late appeal. Only a few decisions cannot be appealed further ('excluded decisions').

There is a one-month time limit for applying, although this can be extended.

Box A
Appeals to the Upper Tribunal

- Appeals to the Upper Tribunal can only be on the basis of an error of law.

- Upper Tribunal appeals are more legalistic and can seem more formal than the First-tier Tribunal – eg, the decision maker is represented by a lawyer. However, unnecessary formality is supposed to be avoided.

- All parties to the appeal have the right of further appeal to the Upper Tribunal.

- It is advisable to have the statement of reasons for the tribunal's decision before trying to appeal to the Upper Tribunal.

- You must apply for permission to appeal first. Your application must initially be made to the First-tier Tribunal, within the time limit.

- Decisions of the Upper Tribunal are binding on all decision makers and the First-tier Tribunal – they therefore affect all claimants, not just your individual case.

Note: if the decision maker intends to appeal further and gives you written notice of this, payment of your benefit that was awarded after the tribunal decision can be suspended.

The Upper Tribunal is generally much less concerned with the particular facts and evidence in your case and much more concerned with the interpretation of the law. The 'submissions' made for the decision maker are drawn up by lawyers. However, the Upper Tribunal has procedural rules that are similar to those that apply to the First-tier Tribunal. In particular, the 'overriding objective' is to deal with cases 'fairly and justly', which includes avoiding unnecessary formality. Parties should be able to participate fully in the proceedings, and have the right to appoint a 'representative', who need not be legally qualified.

Do you need a representative?

You are not required to have a 'representative' for an appeal to the 'Upper Tribunal'. However, appeals to the Upper Tribunal are much more concerned with legal argument than most appeals to the 'First-tier Tribunal', and sometimes these can be complex. If you are not experienced in dealing with social security law, it is therefore advisable to find a representative or, at least, get detailed advice. The 'decision maker' is represented by a legally qualified person.

Which decisions are excluded?

Some decisions cannot be appealed to the 'Upper Tribunal'. These are mainly decisions the 'First-tier Tribunal' makes about reviewing an earlier decision it made. Also, you cannot appeal against a decision of the First-tier Tribunal to refer a matter to the Upper Tribunal. In these cases, you can apply to the Upper Tribunal for a 'judicial review' of the decision.

What is an error of law?

There is no strict definition of an 'error of law' in a tribunal decision. It is a matter of judgement, taking into account the precise wording of the decision and the 'statement of reasons', and applying some general principles to that.

The fact that you disagree with the decision, or that someone else could have come to a different decision on the same facts, is not, in itself, an error of law.

The following are the most common errors of law in tribunal decisions.

- The tribunal gave inadequate reasons for its decision. The tribunal's reasons should enable you to see why it reached the decision it did. Sometimes, the reason for the decision may be obvious and the tribunal does not need to spell everything out. A decision is not wrong just because evidence produced later contradicts it. However, if the tribunal relied on a particular piece of evidence, or preferred one piece of evidence over another, it should say why.

- The tribunal made inadequate 'findings of fact' (ie, deciding the facts that were relevant to your appeal) for its decision, or the facts it found are such that it could not reasonably and correctly have made the decision that it did. The tribunal must establish sufficient facts to support its decision. If facts are disputed, the tribunal should say which version it prefers and why.

- The tribunal applied the law incorrectly – eg, it misinterpreted the wording in a particular part of the 'work capability assessment' or in the test for personal independence payment and so did not award you the correct points.

Other errors of law are possible, although are less common.

- The tribunal 'breached the rules of natural justice'. See Box B for what this means.

- The tribunal did not provide a statement of reasons for its decision when it had a duty to do so.

- The tribunal took things into account which it should not have, or refused to take into account things which it should have.

- The tribunal conducted a physical examination and based its decision on that (except in an industrial injuries benefit case).

> Box B
> **Natural justice**
>
> The idea of 'natural justice' is a broad one, but essentially it means that each 'party to the appeal' must be given a fair chance to put her/his case. The specific requirement for a tribunal to deal with a case 'fairly and justly' is part of this.
>
> Showing that a tribunal has breached the rules on natural justice can be difficult, as much depends on the facts of your case – getting the 'record of proceedings' may help. Examples can include if the tribunal held the hearing in your absence even though you intended to be there. The fact that you found the tribunal abrupt or unfriendly is not enough.

4. Appealing to the Upper Tribunal

How do you apply for permission to appeal?

You must apply to the 'First-tier Tribunal' for permission to appeal to the 'Upper Tribunal'. If you are refused, you can apply directly to the Upper Tribunal.

The 'decision maker' can also apply for permission to appeal. If the decision maker applies for permission to appeal within the time limit, payment of any benefit awarded to you as a result of the tribunal decision can be suspended.

The judge who considers your application for permission to appeal to the Upper Tribunal may not be the same judge who was on the tribunal that heard your appeal.

What decisions can the First-tier tribunal make?

The judge can do any of the following.

- Review the 'First-tier Tribunal' decision, if s/he is satisfied that there is an 'error of law' in it. This only applies in very clear cases, and is not common.

- Grant you permission to appeal. You are notified of this, and you must then send a 'notice of appeal' to the 'Upper Tribunal' so that it is received within one month of your being sent the permission to appeal. You are sent Form UT1 on which to do this. The Upper Tribunal can extend the time limit, but does not have to. If you send the notice of appeal late, explain why. You should include the notice granting you permission to appeal and a copy of the tribunal's decision and 'statement of reasons' (if you have one).

- Refuse you permission to appeal. You must be notified of this in writing, along with a statement of reasons for the refusal and notice of your right to apply directly to the Upper Tribunal for permission to appeal.

If there is no statement of reasons for the tribunal's decision because no one has applied for one, the judge must first treat your application as an application for a statement of reasons. If a statement of reasons is then provided, you must apply for permission to appeal again. If a statement of reasons is refused (eg, because you apply outside the time limit), the judge can either refuse you permission to appeal or grant it.

Has the judge reviewed the decision?

If the judge reviews the decision, you must be notified of the outcome and of any further right of appeal you may have. The judge can:

- correct accidental errors in the decision
- amend the reasons given for the decision (but not add new reasons the tribunal had not previously considered)
- 'set aside' (cancel) the decision. The tribunal must then either make a new decision or refer it to the Upper Tribunal

Generally, you cannot appeal against a decision to review (or not to review) the decision of the tribunal. However, you may be able to appeal if the review results in an accidental error being corrected or the reasons amended.

If the decision is set aside and a new decision made by the First-tier Tribunal, you have the same right of appeal as you had with the original decision. You can apply for a statement of reasons and ask for permission to appeal.

Has the First-tier Tribunal refused you permission to appeal?

If the judge refuses to give you permission to appeal to the 'Upper Tribunal', you can reapply directly to the Upper Tribunal. Your application should be received by the Upper Tribunal no later than one month after the date the 'First-tier Tribunal's' refusal was sent. The Upper Tribunal can allow a longer period, but does not have to. If your application is late, explain why.

Your application to the Upper Tribunal should ideally be on Form UT1, available from HM Courts and Tribunals Service. You do not have to use the form, but your application must be in writing. It must include your details and those of your 'representative' and identify the First-tier Tribunal decision you are appealing. It must also include:

- the alleged 'error of law' in the decision
- copies of the decision, the 'statement of reasons' (if you have one) and the notice of the First-tier Tribunal's refusal to grant you permission to appeal
- the reasons why you are late in applying for permission to appeal, if applicable

However, the Upper Tribunal can ignore any irregularities in your application. If you do not have a statement of reasons, the Upper Tribunal can still grant you permission to appeal. You must still show that there is an error of law in the tribunal's decision – and this is more difficult without a statement of reasons. If the tribunal does not provide a statement of reasons when it has a duty to do so (ie, if you requested one within the one-month time limit), this, in itself, is an error of law.

What can the Upper Tribunal do?

The 'Upper Tribunal' decides whether or not to grant you permission to appeal and sends you written notice of this.

If you are given permission, your appeal goes ahead and the Upper Tribunal considers whether or not to 'allow' it. It can either decide there was no 'error of law', so that the decision of the 'First-tier Tribunal' stands, or to allow the appeal because the decision contains an error of law. In this case, the Upper Tribunal either decides itself what the correct decision should have been or 'sets aside' (cancels) the First-tier Tribunal's decision and orders a new tribunal to reconsider the appeal.

The Upper Tribunal may hold an 'oral hearing' of your application for permission to appeal or the appeal itself. In most cases, oral hearings are not held.

If you are refused permission by the Upper Tribunal, this means your appeal does not go ahead. You cannot appeal any further.

It may be possible to apply to a court for a 'judicial review' of the refusal. Judicial review is a court process in which a judge reviews the lawfulness of a decision against which you do not have another right of appeal. However, judicial review of an Upper Tribunal decision refusing you permission to appeal is only possible in cases that are thought to have an important point of principle or practice or some other compelling reason, as the Upper Tribunal is regarded as an expert court. You must apply no more than 16 days after you were notified of the Upper Tribunal's decision. Judicial review can involve legal costs. You may need the services of a solicitor or legal advice centre to apply for a judicial review. Before making any application, get advice about what you might have to pay.

Otherwise, the decision of the Upper Tribunal is final. In the vast majority of cases, the refusal of the Upper Tribunal to grant permission is the final decision.

Judicial review in the Upper Tribunal

In a few cases, there is no right of appeal to the 'Upper Tribunal' against a decision of the 'First-tier Tribunal'. These are where the tribunal has made an 'excluded decision', such as a decision to review its own earlier decision. It may be possible to apply for a 'judicial review' of the excluded decision and have that considered by the Upper Tribunal, although in practice this is rare. Judicial reviews can involve legal costs, so get advice from a solicitor about what you might have to pay. In Scotland, you must apply first to the Court of Session, which may then transfer your application to the Upper Tribunal.

Appealing to the higher courts

Decisions of the 'Upper Tribunal' can sometimes be the subject of further appeals. These appeals are to the higher courts – the Court of Appeal in England and Wales and the Court of Session in Scotland. Such appeals can only be on the basis of an 'error of law' in the Upper Tribunal's decision and are wholly concerned with legal argument. After that, still further appeals are possible, again on the basis of an error of law, to the Supreme Court and finally to the European courts. Appeals to the higher courts can involve legal costs and you should consider obtaining legal advice from a solicitor. Before making any application, get advice about what you might have to pay.

Further information

There is more information about appeals to the Upper Tribunal and the courts in CPAG's *Welfare Benefits and Tax Credits Handbook*.

Appendix

Glossary of terms

Adjourned/adjournment

A pause in an appeal hearing – eg, to allow one party to the appeal to consider a new point or to get more evidence.

Allow

The tribunal agrees, at least in part, that the decision being appealed is wrong.

Appointee

Someone, usually a relative, who is authorised by the Department for Work and Pensions or HM Revenue and Customs to claim benefits or tax credits on another person's behalf if s/he cannot claim for her/himself – eg, perhaps because of a learning disability.

Budgeting advance

An advance payment of universal credit in the form of a loan, usually for people who have been on benefits for at least six months.

Claimant

The person who has made an appeal.

Clearance time

The time it takes for an appeal to be heard and decided by the appeal tribunal.

Couple

Two people living together who are married or civil partners, or who are living together as if they were married or civil partners.

Daily living component

The part of personal independence payment paid if you have problems with daily living activities, or are terminally ill.

Decision maker

An officer in the Department for Work and Pensions, HM Revenue and Customs or local authority who makes the original decision concerning entitlement to benefit or tax credits, and who considers a request for the decision to be looked at again.

Decision notice
A short written summary of the tribunal's decision. Also, the letter from the decision maker, informing you of the decision about your benefit or tax credit claim.

Descriptor
A statement used for personal independence payment, describing your ability to carry out one of the specific daily living or mobility activities.

Direct lodgement
Sending the appeal directly to HM Courts and Tribunals Service, rather than to the decision maker.

Direction
An order from the tribunal requiring something to be done.

Domicilary hearing
An oral hearing of an appeal heard in the claimant's home, rather than at a tribunal venue.

Error of law
A legal mistake in the tribunal's decision.

Expediting
The process by which the tribunal clerk speeds up the arrangement of an appeal hearing so that it is heard earlier than it might otherwise have been.

Findings of fact
The facts established and recorded by a tribunal that are relevant to the appeal.

First-tier Tribunal
The independent tribunal that considers appeals against benefit and tax credit decisions made by the Department for Work and Pensions, HM Revenue and Customs and local authorities.

Grounds
The reasons for the appeal.

Hardship payments
Reduced-rate payments of jobseeker's allowance, employment and support allowance and universal credit that are made in limited circumstances.

HM Courts and Tribunals Service
The body that administers and conducts the independent hearing of an appeal.

Judicial review
A way of challenging in court the decisions of government departments, local authorities and some tribunals against which there is no right of appeal.

Lapse
The process of replacing a decision being appealed before the appeal is heard.

Limited capability for work
A test of whether a person's ability to work is limited by a health condition.

Limited capability for work element
An amount included in universal credit for people whose ability to work is limited by a health condition.

Limited capability for work-related activity
A test of how severe a person's health problems are and whether her/his ability to prepare for work is limited.

Mandatory reconsideration
The requirement to have a decision looked at again, via a revision (for benefits) or a review (for tax credits), by the decision maker before an appeal can be made.

Mandatory reconsideration notice
The letter in which the outcome of a mandatory reconsideration is sent to the claimant.

Means-tested benefit
A benefit that is only paid if someone's income and capital are low enough.

Mobility component
The part of disability living allowance or personal independence payment paid if you have mobility problems.

Natural justice
The concept that includes allowing each party to the appeal to be given a fair chance to put her/his case.

Non-contributory benefit
A benefit for which entitlement does not depend on having paid a certain amount of national insurance contributions.

Non-means-tested benefit
A benefit that is paid regardless of the amount of someone's income or capital.

Official error
An error by, for example, someone at the Department for Work and Pensions, HM Revenue and Customs or a local authority which results in a benefit decision being wrong.

Oral hearing
A hearing of an appeal in which the person who made the appeal is present and is asked questions by the tribunal.

Overpayment
An amount of benefit that is paid which is more than a person's entitlement.

Paper hearing
A consideration of an appeal without an oral hearing using just the appeal papers.

Parties to the appeal
The person who has made the appeal and the body which made the decision being appealed.

Presenting officer
A representative from the body which made the decision being appealed who attends an oral hearing to assist the tribunal.

Postponed/postponement
Putting off a tribunal hearing, before it has started, so that it begins on a later date.

Record of proceedings
The notes made of a tribunal hearing by the judge, or an electronic recording of the hearing, recording the submission, evidence and procedural matters such as any consideration of adjournment.

Representative
Someone who helps a claimant to put her/his case to the tribunal.

Review
A statutory method that allows tax credit decisions to be changed.

Revision
A statutory method that allows benefit decisions to be changed.

Right to reside
A social security test, mainly affecting European Economic Area nationals, which must be satisfied in order to claim certain benefits.

Sanction
A reduction in a person's benefit award for failing to meet certain work-related requirements.

Secretary of State for Work and Pensions
The government minister with overall responsibility for the Department for Work and Pensions. Formally speaking, the person who makes decisons on benefits administered by the Department.

Set aside
Cancelling a tribunal decision on certain grounds.

Short-term advance
An advance of universal credit which can be paid if someone is in hardship while waiting for her/his first payment.

Slips of the pen
Minor accidental errors in a tribunal's written decision, which can be corrected by the tribunal.

Social Entitlement Chamber
The part of HM Courts and Tribunals Service that deals with appeals about benefits and tax credits.

Social Security and Child Support Commissioner
The independent judicial body that previously considered further appeals against tribunal decisions.

Statement of reasons
A written statement from the tribunal explaining why it came to its decision.

Struck out
When an appeal is cancelled before it has been considered.

Submission
An argument or setting out a case, usually in writing, which is put to the tribunal.

Supersession
A statutory method of allowing benefit decisions to be changed, usually as a result of a change in circumstances.

Support component
An amount included in employment and support allowance for people who have limited capability for work-related activity. If someone gets this, s/he is referred to as being in the 'support group'.

Tribunal clerk
The official responsible for administering an appeal, including arranging the hearing and providing administrative support to the tribunal.

Uphold
Allow an appeal – ie, agree, at least in part, that the decision is wrong.

Upper Tribunal
The independent judicial body that considers further appeals against decisions of tribunals.

Waive
Where the tribunal uses its legal discretion so that it does not insist that a procedural rule be observed.

Weighing evidence
The process by which a tribunal decides how much it should be influenced by a particular piece of evidence in coming to its decision.

Work capability assessment
A social security test used to decide whether someone is too ill to work.

Work-focused interview
A compulsory interview with the Department for Work and Pensions to discuss job opportunities, barriers to work and training.

Work-related activity component
An amount included in employment and support allowance for people whose ability to work is limited.

Index